Altered Creatures Epic Fantasy Adventures

Art of the Altered Creatures

Illustrations by Steve Ott

Read free stories and
further Adventures of Thorik Dain at
www.AlteredCreatures.com

Copyright © 2015 by Anthony G. Wedgeworth
Published by Anthony G. Wedgeworth
Illustrations by Steve Ott

ISBN-13: 978-1511512985
ISBN-10: 1511512989

Art of the Altered Creatures
AC Epic Fantasy Adventure Art Series
Book 1, Revision 1.00
www.AlteredCreatures.com

No thrashers or Chuttlebeast were harmed in the making of this book.

Altered Creatures Epic Fantasy Adventures

Art of the Altered Creatures

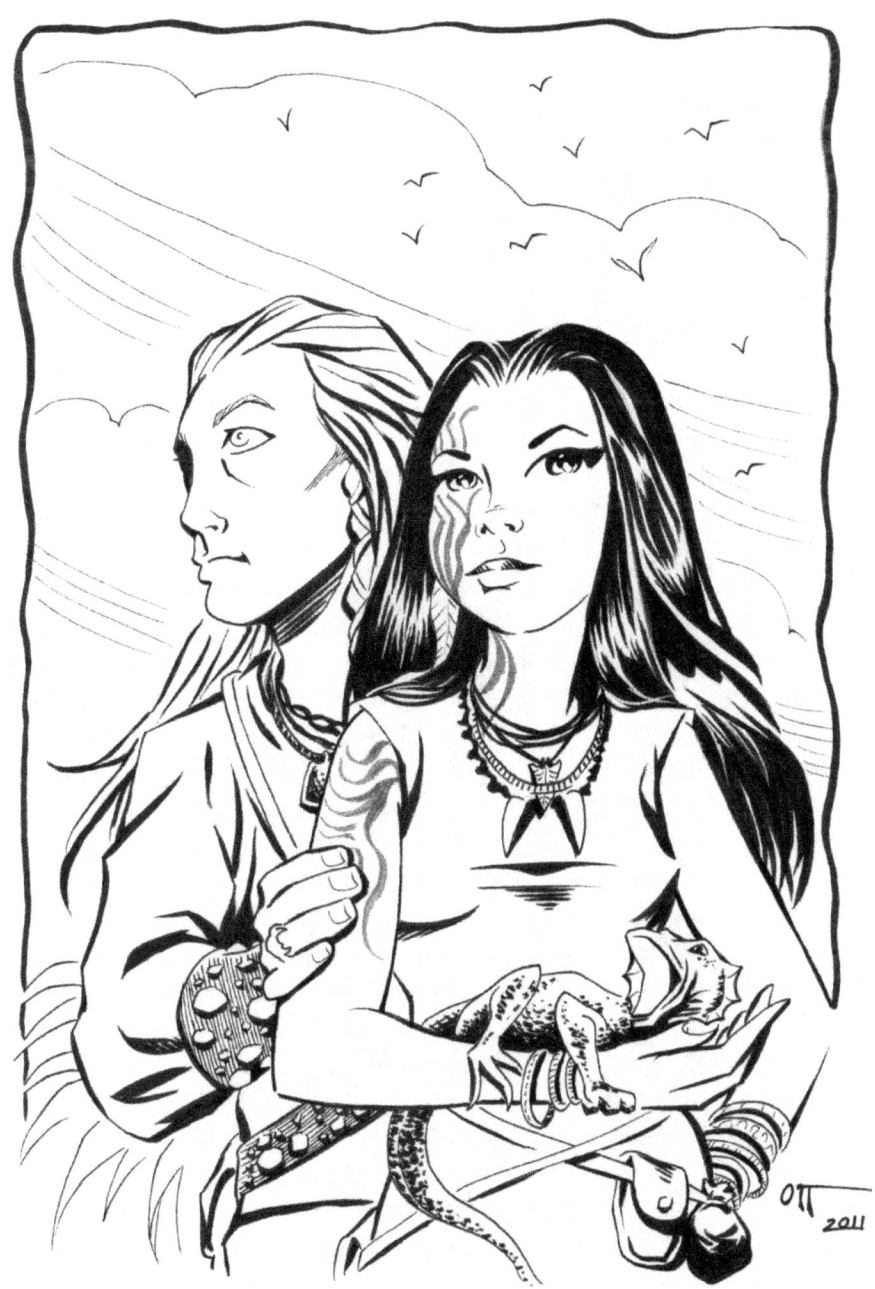

Thorik and Avanda

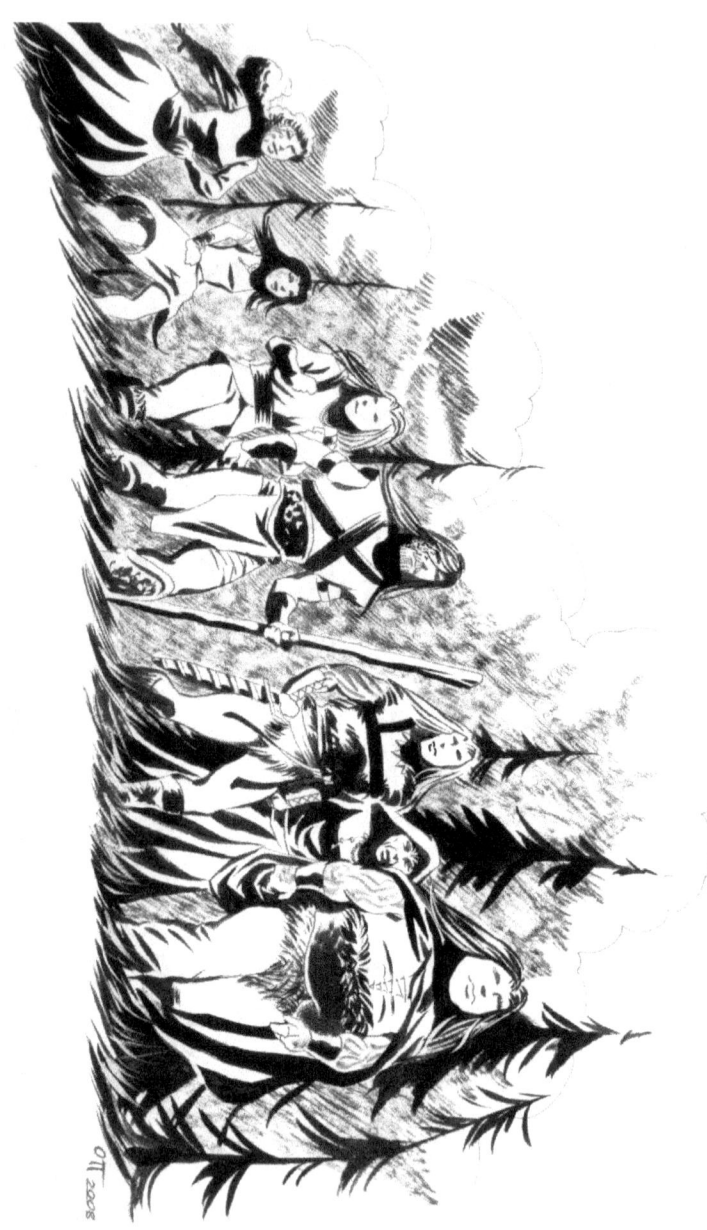

Leaving Farbank

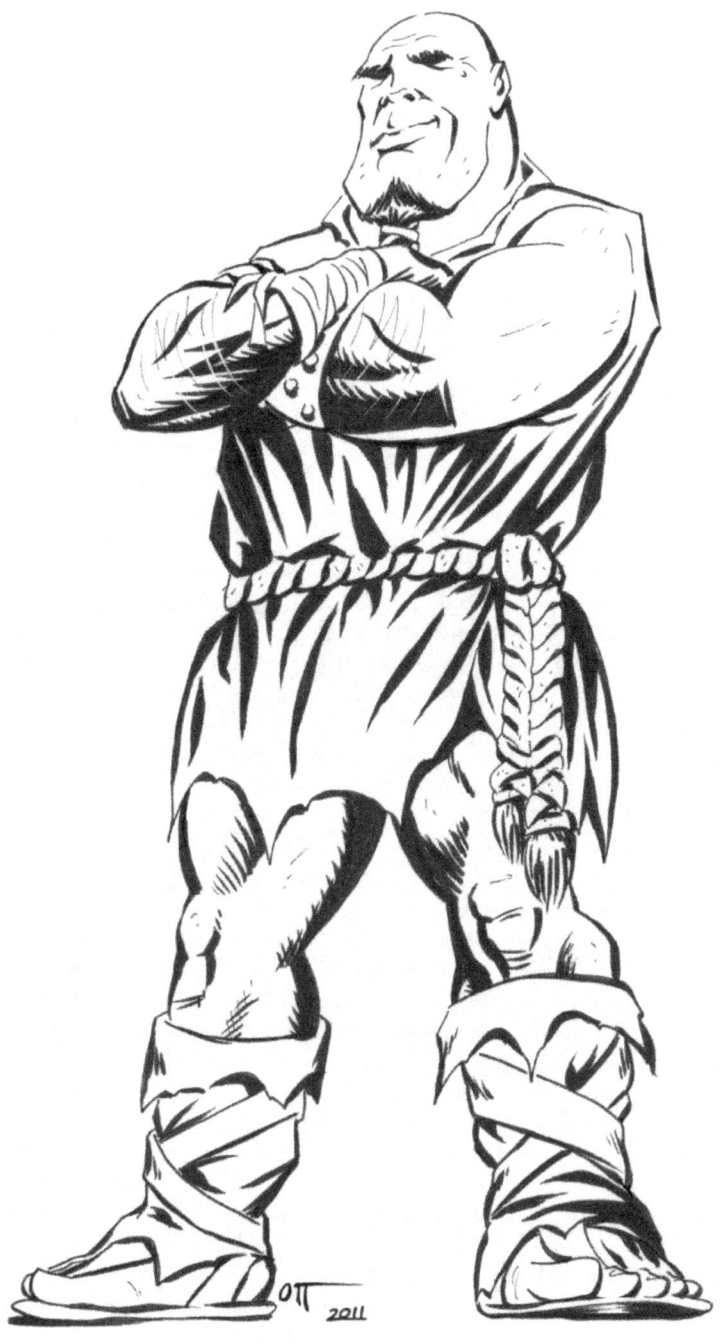

Grewen the giant Mognin

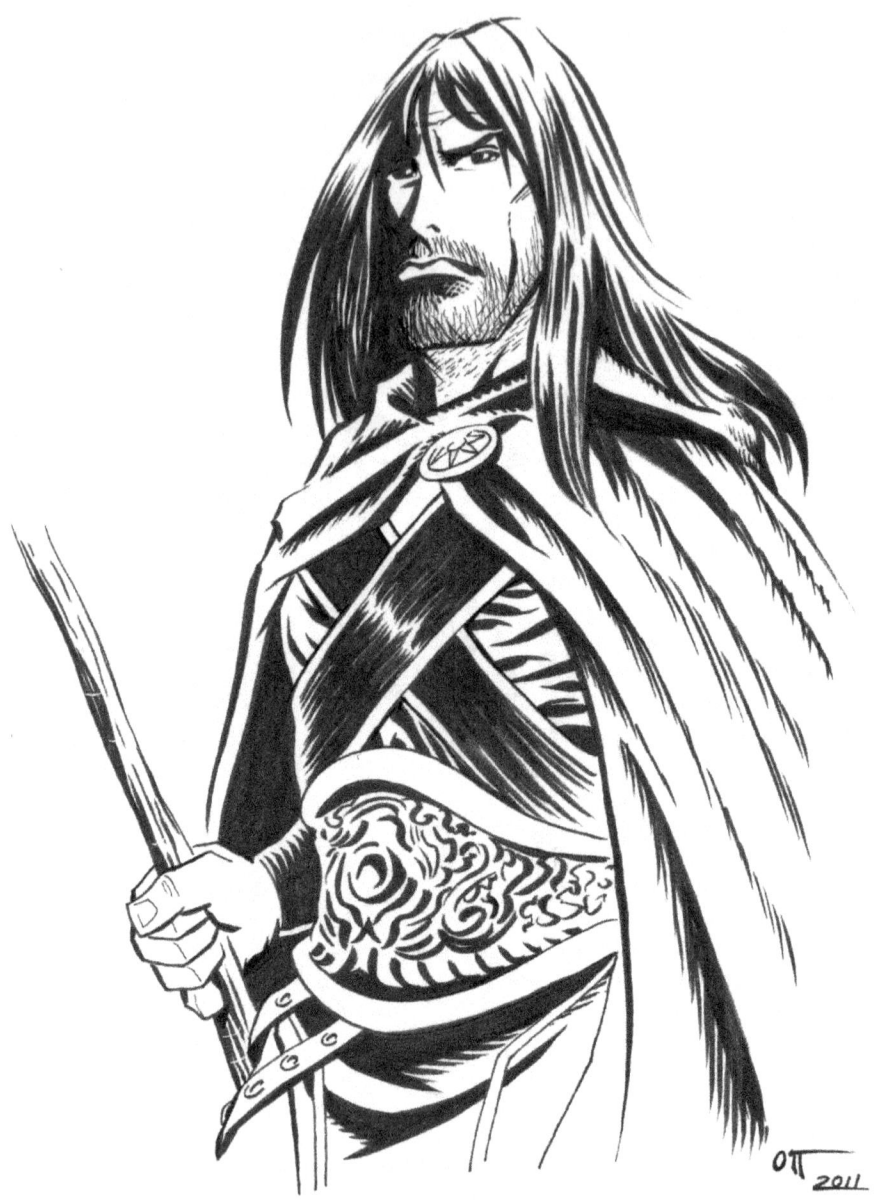

Ambrosius
The E'rudite with magical powers

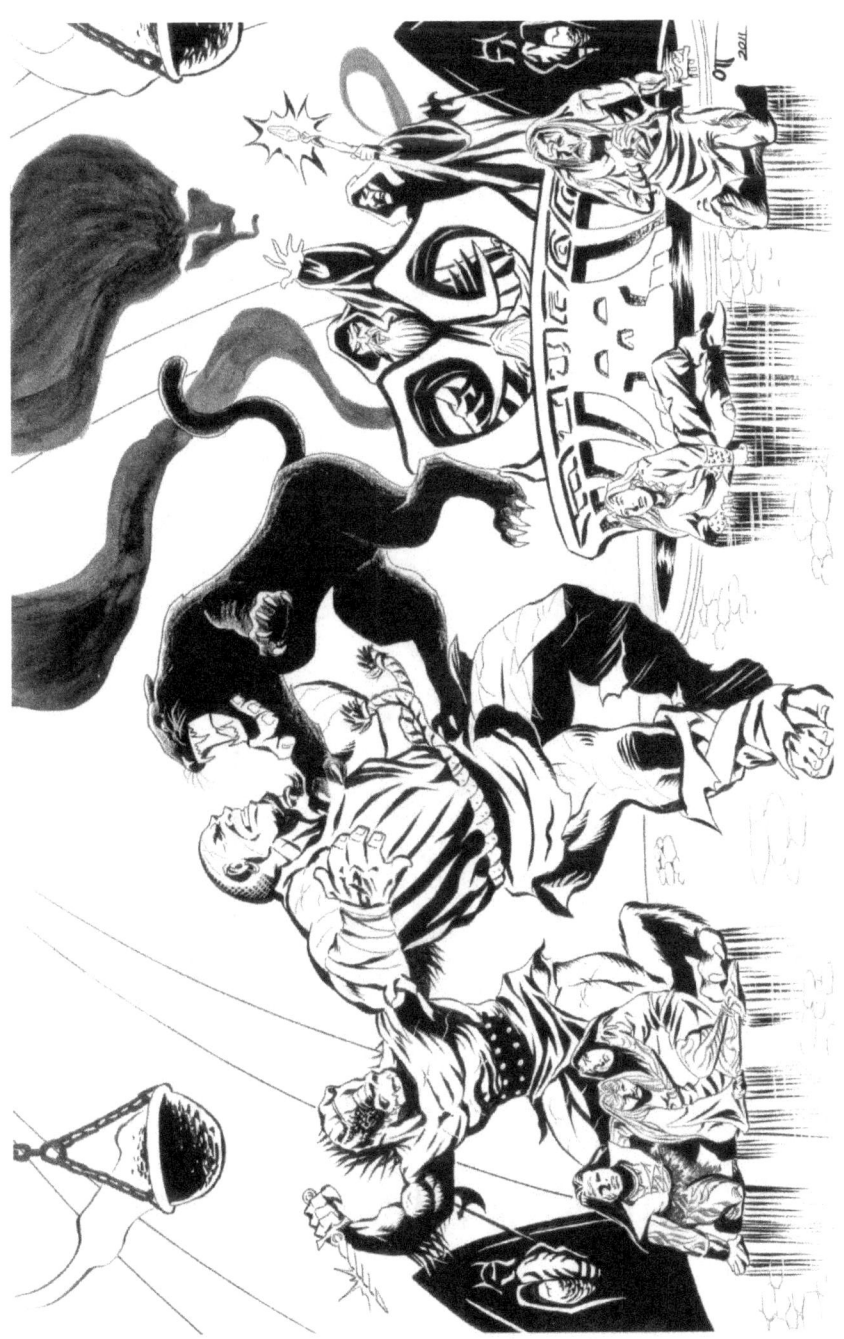

Temple of Sorat

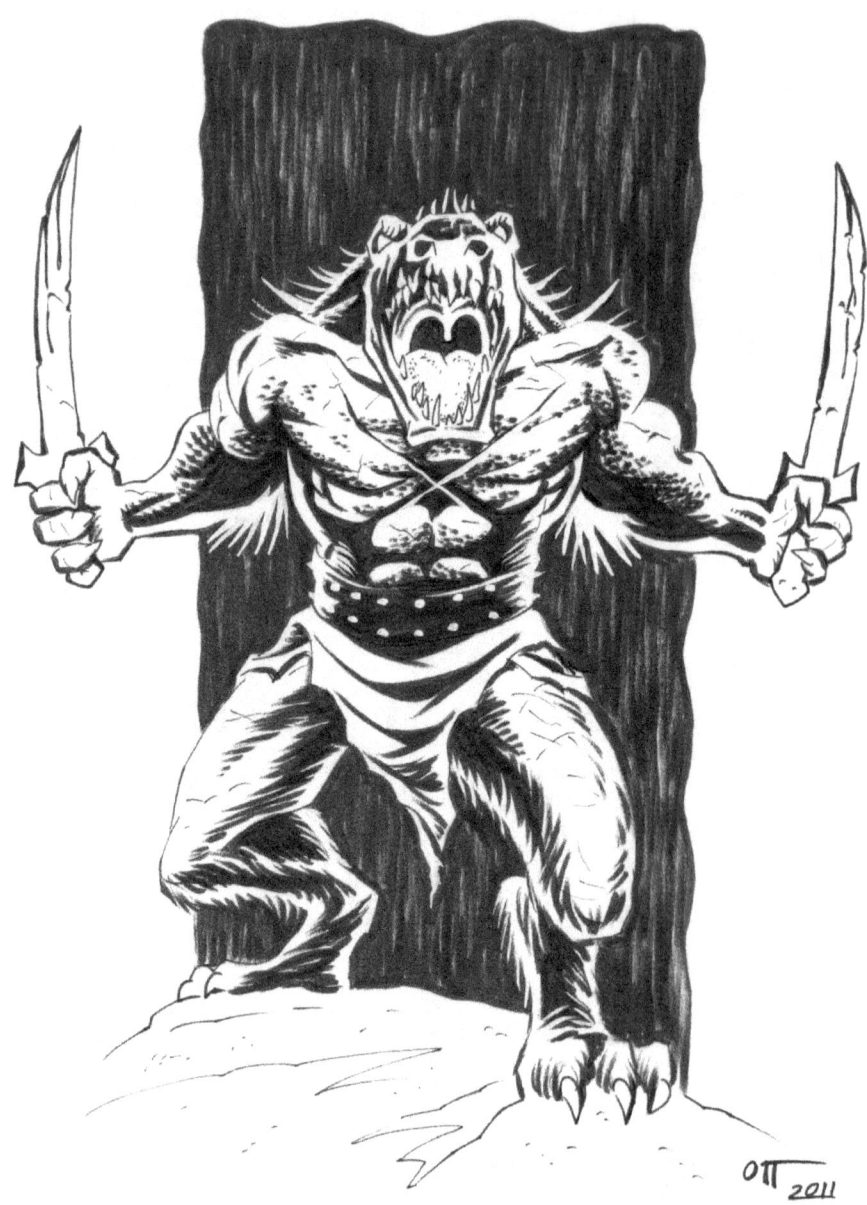

Santorray, the Blothrud

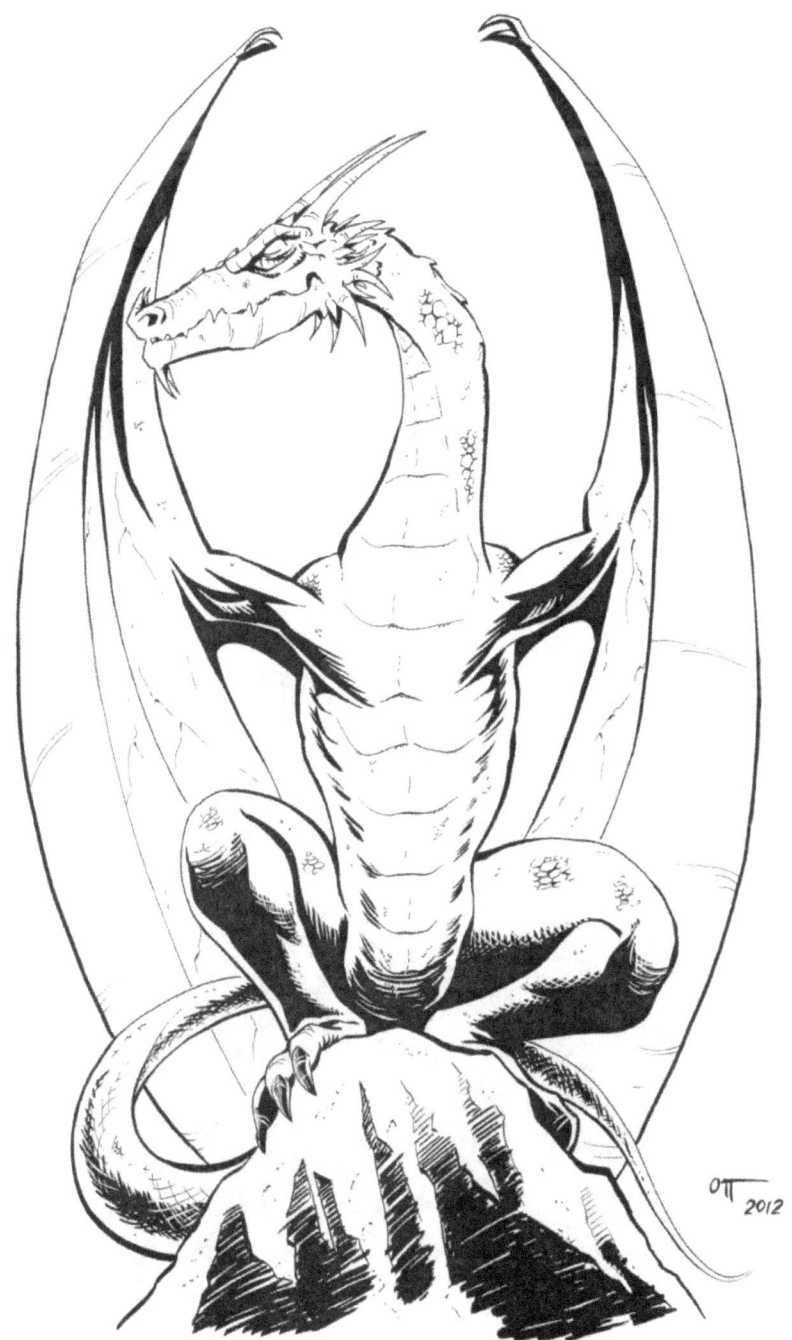

Draq, the red-tipped silver dragon

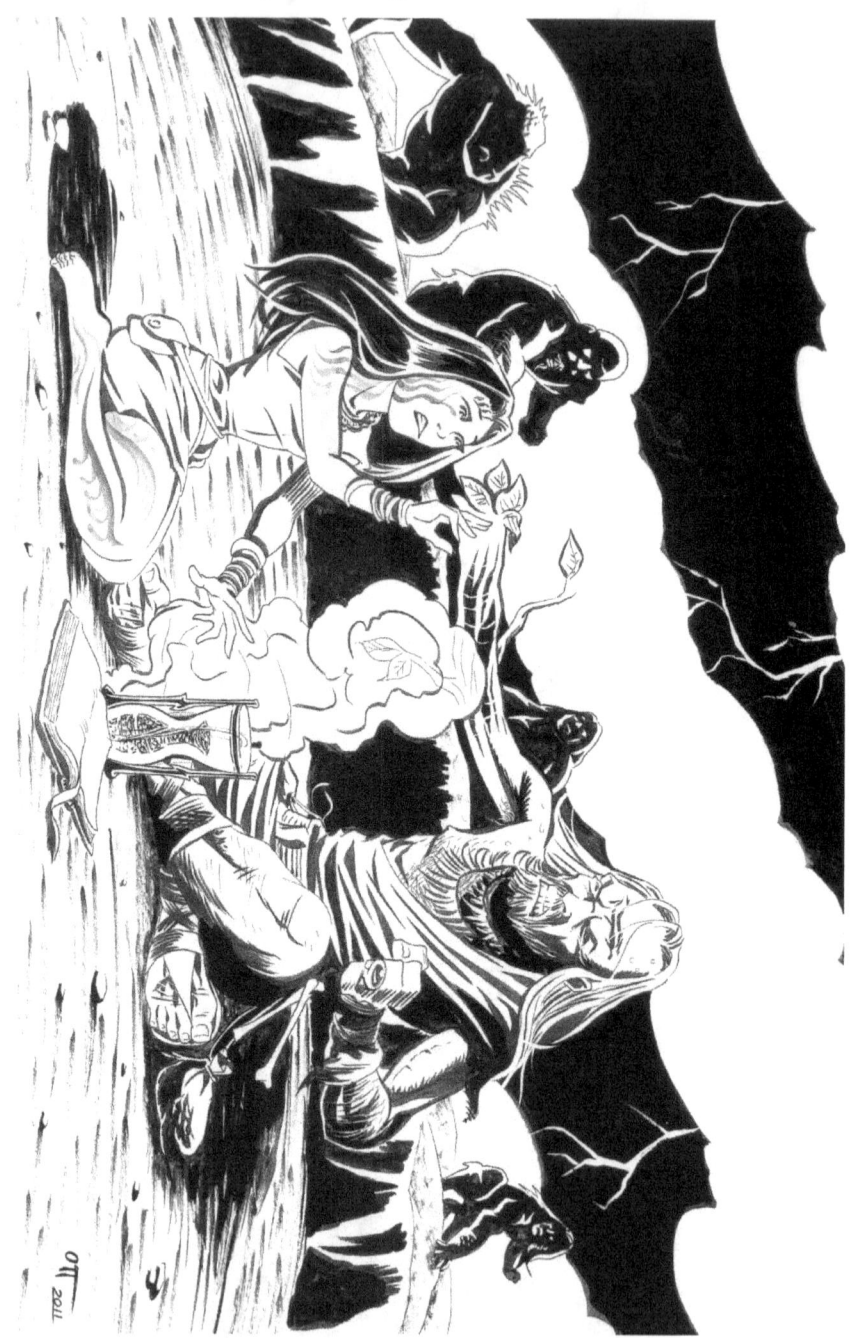

Avanda and Bryus

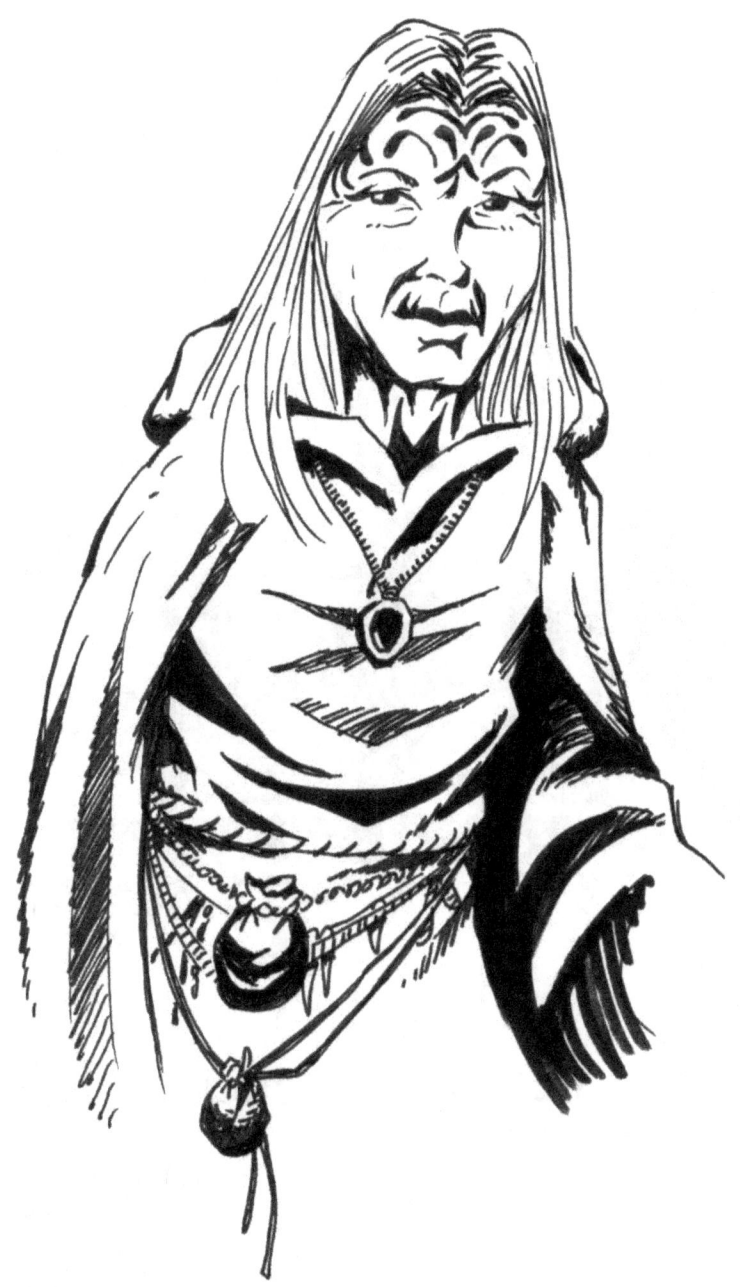

Gluic, Thorik's Grandmother

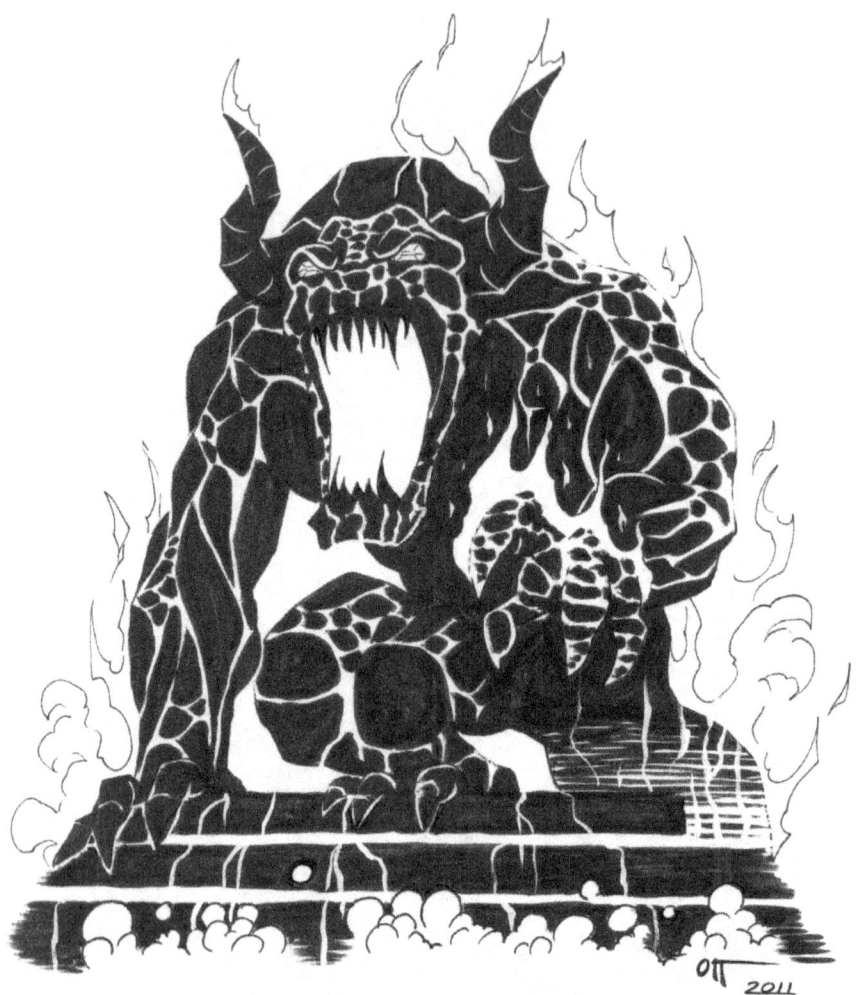

Bakalor
The ruler of the underworld

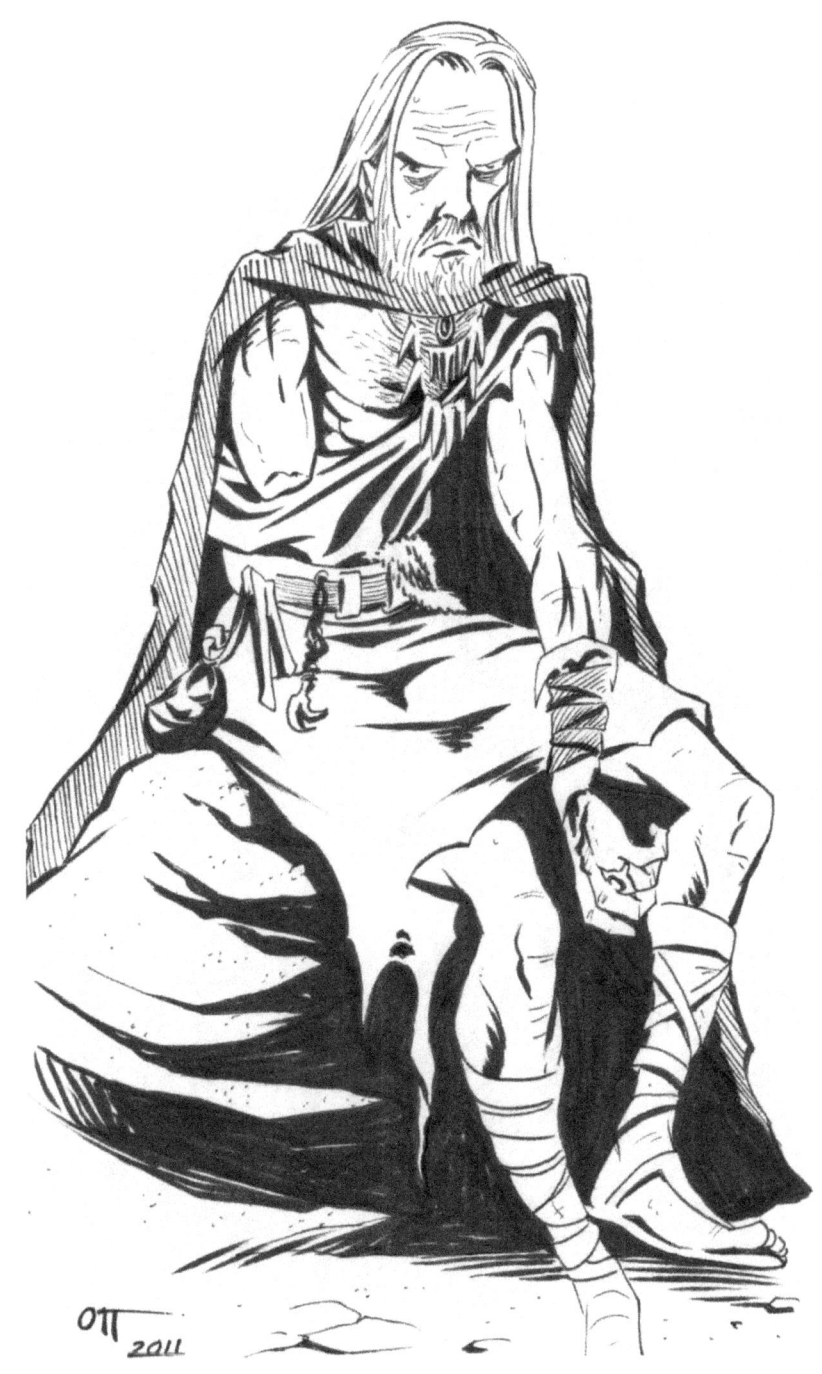

Bryus Grum

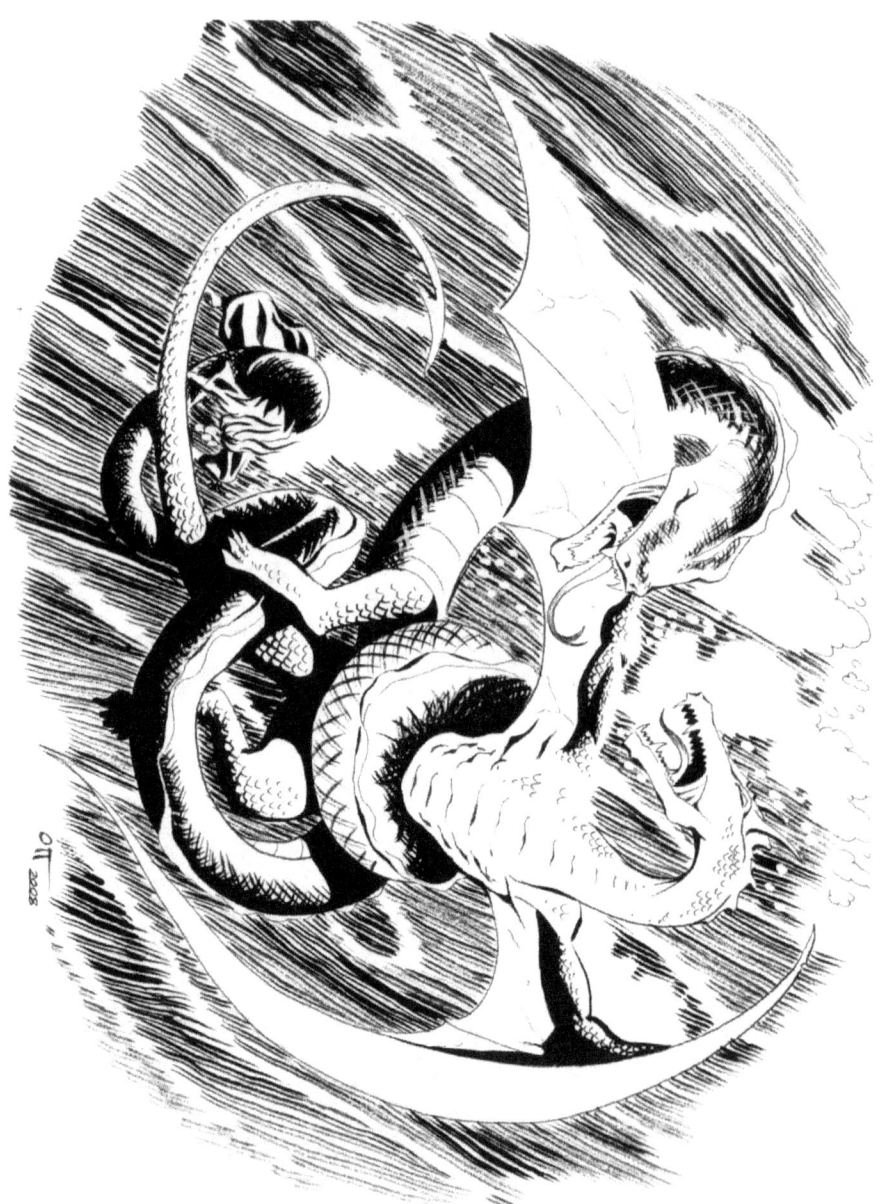

Draq and the Sea Serpent

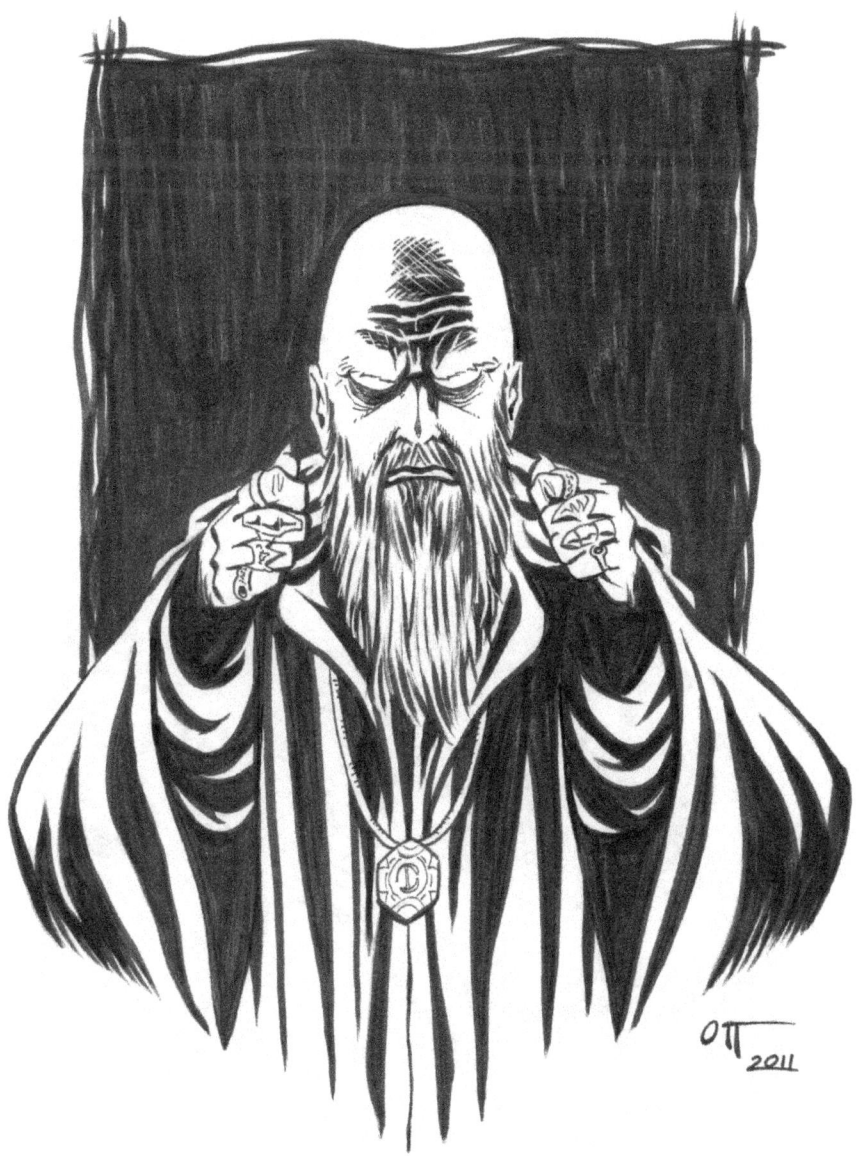

Darkmere

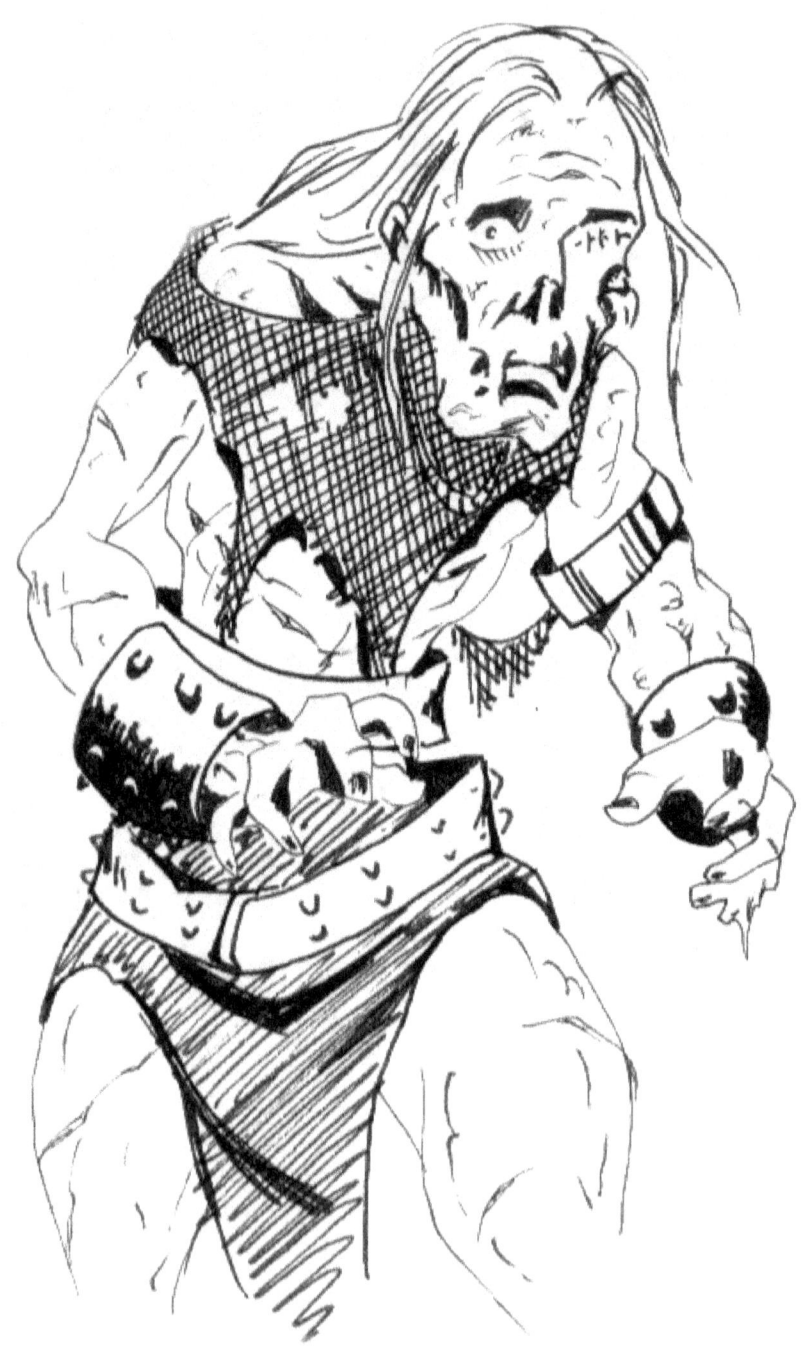

Korin, after the Civil War

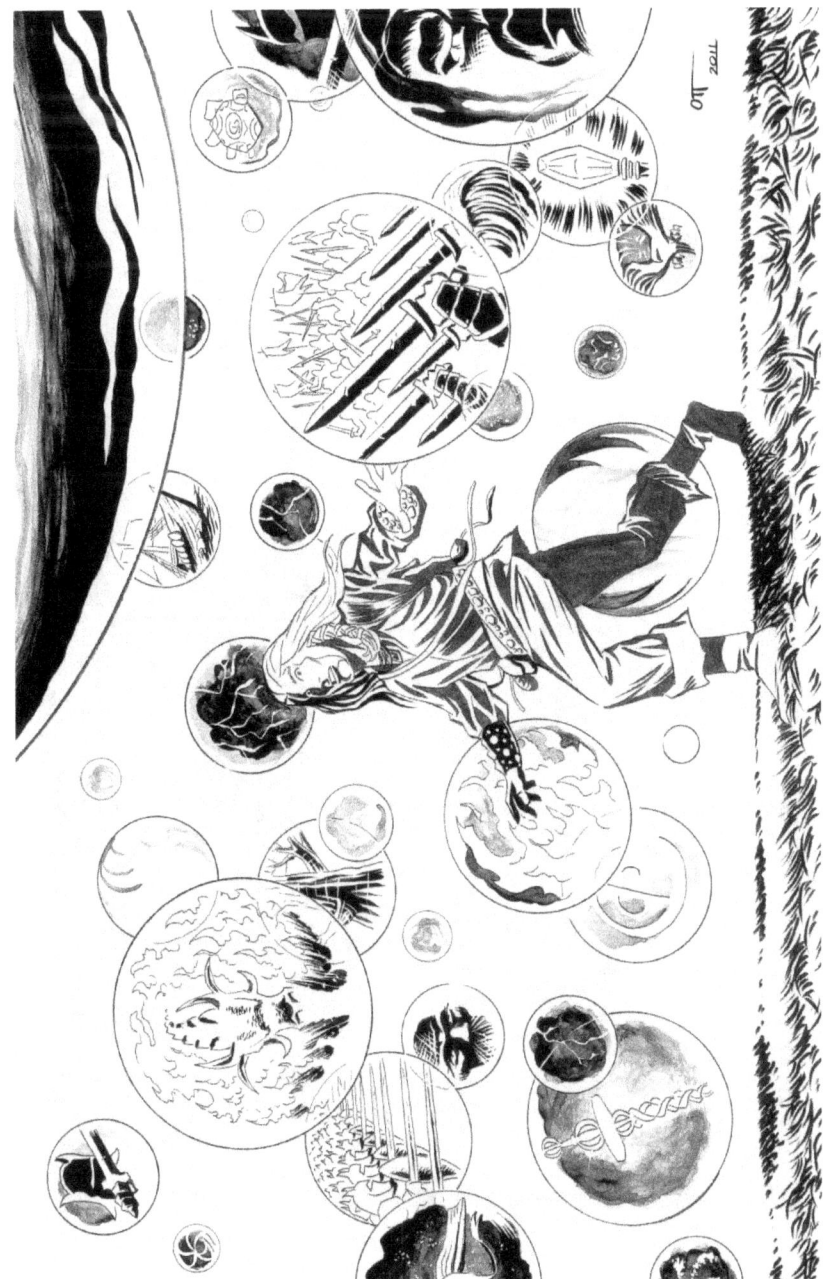

Thorik in the Govi Glade

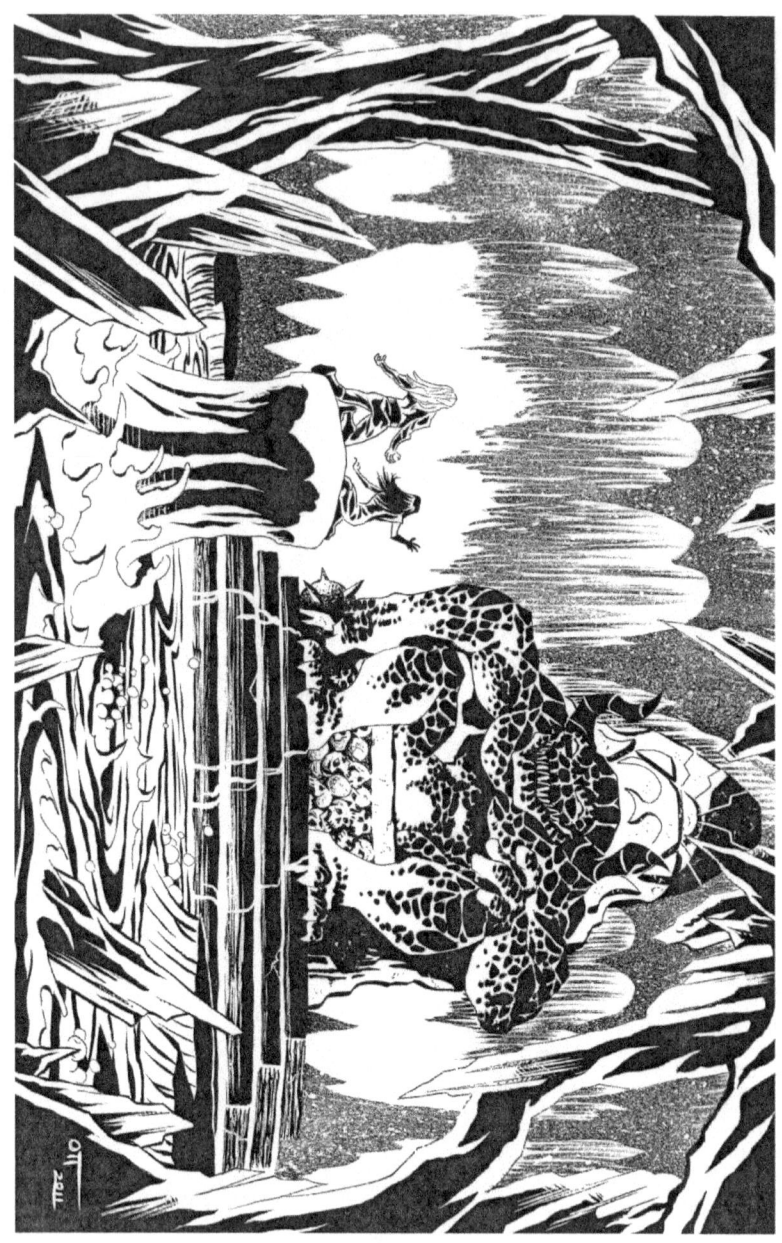

Thorik & Avanda
trapped by Bakalor

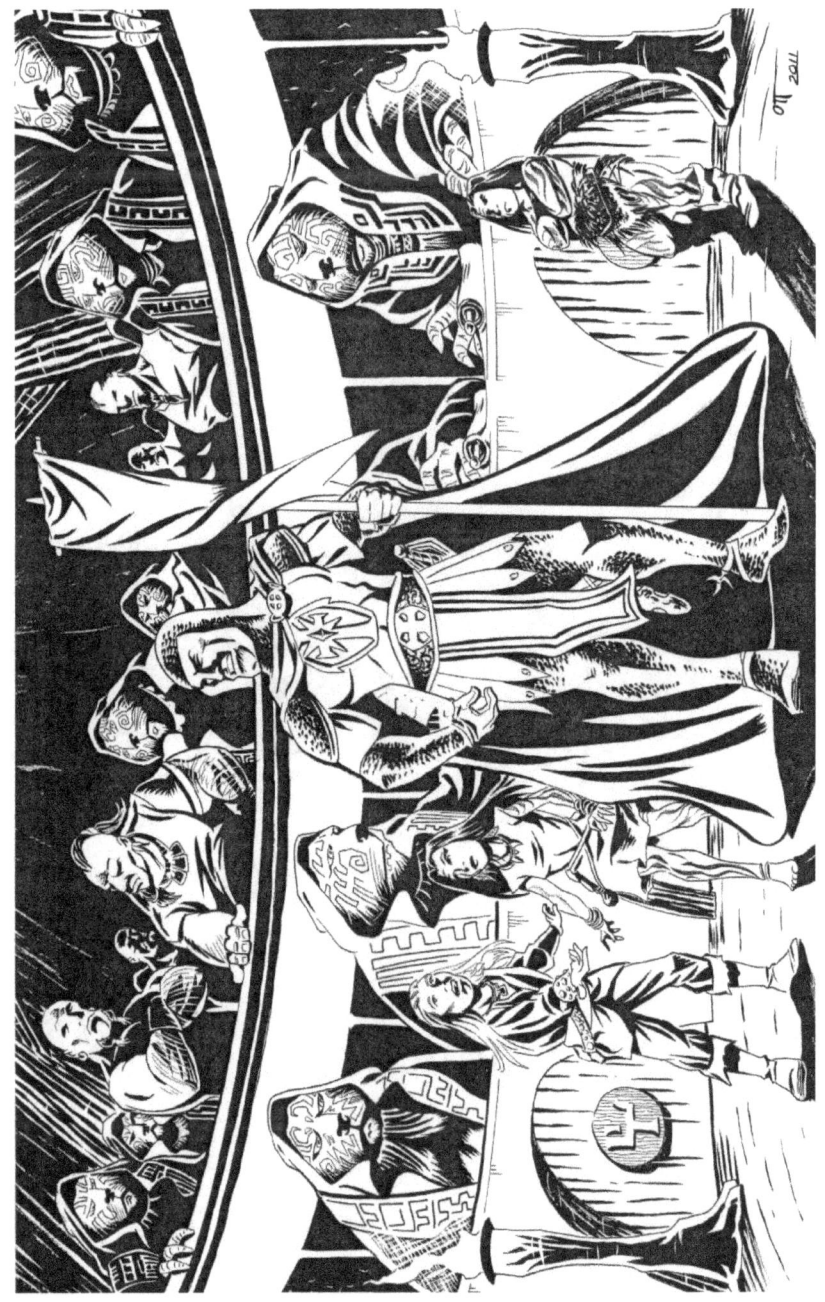

Trewek's High Council

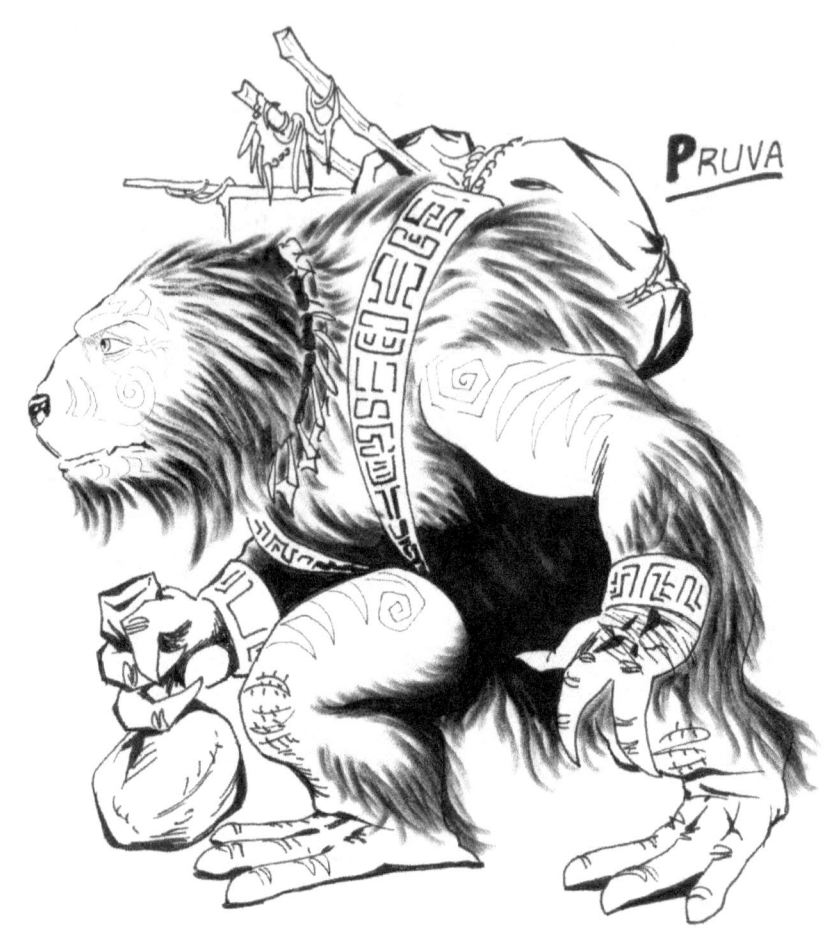

Pruva, the Gathler

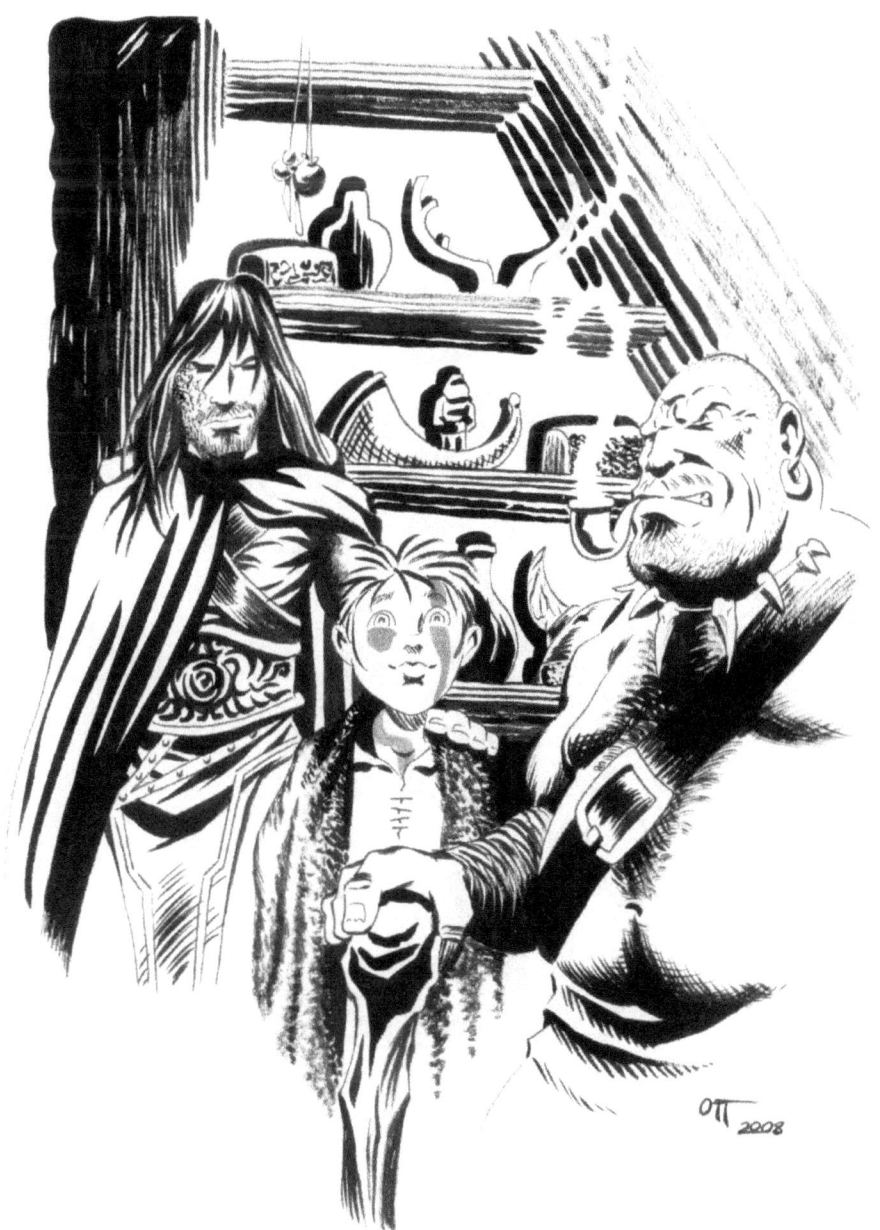

Ambrosius, Bik, and Dare

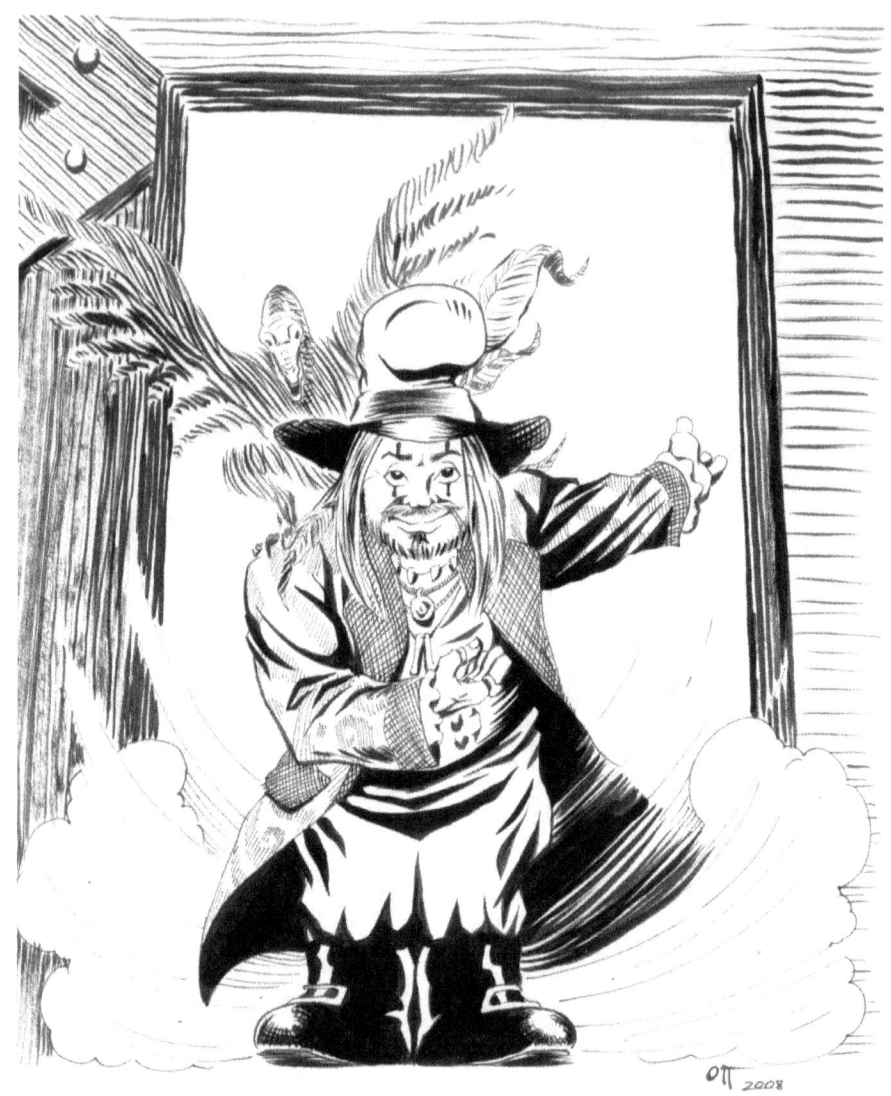

The Thespian
As he enters the
"Dare to Trade" shop

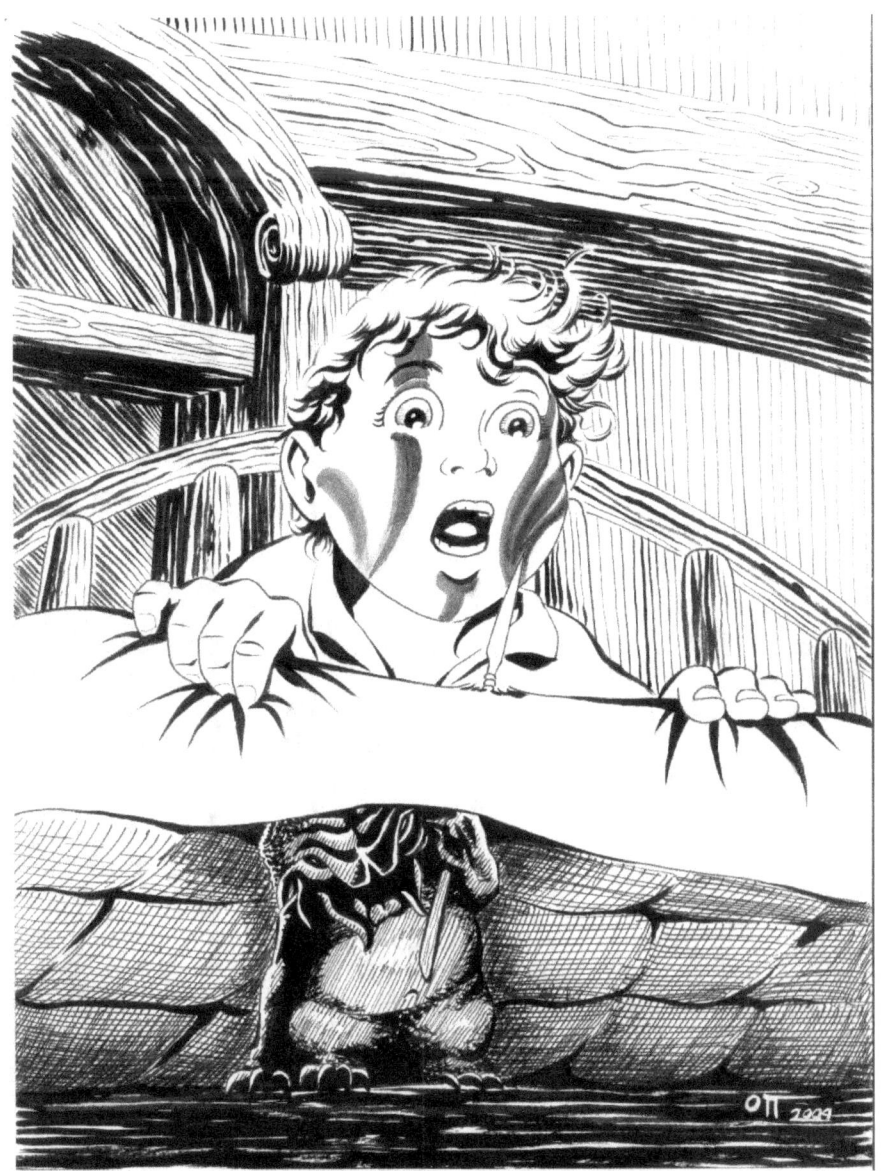

Gaz and the wooden Baka idol

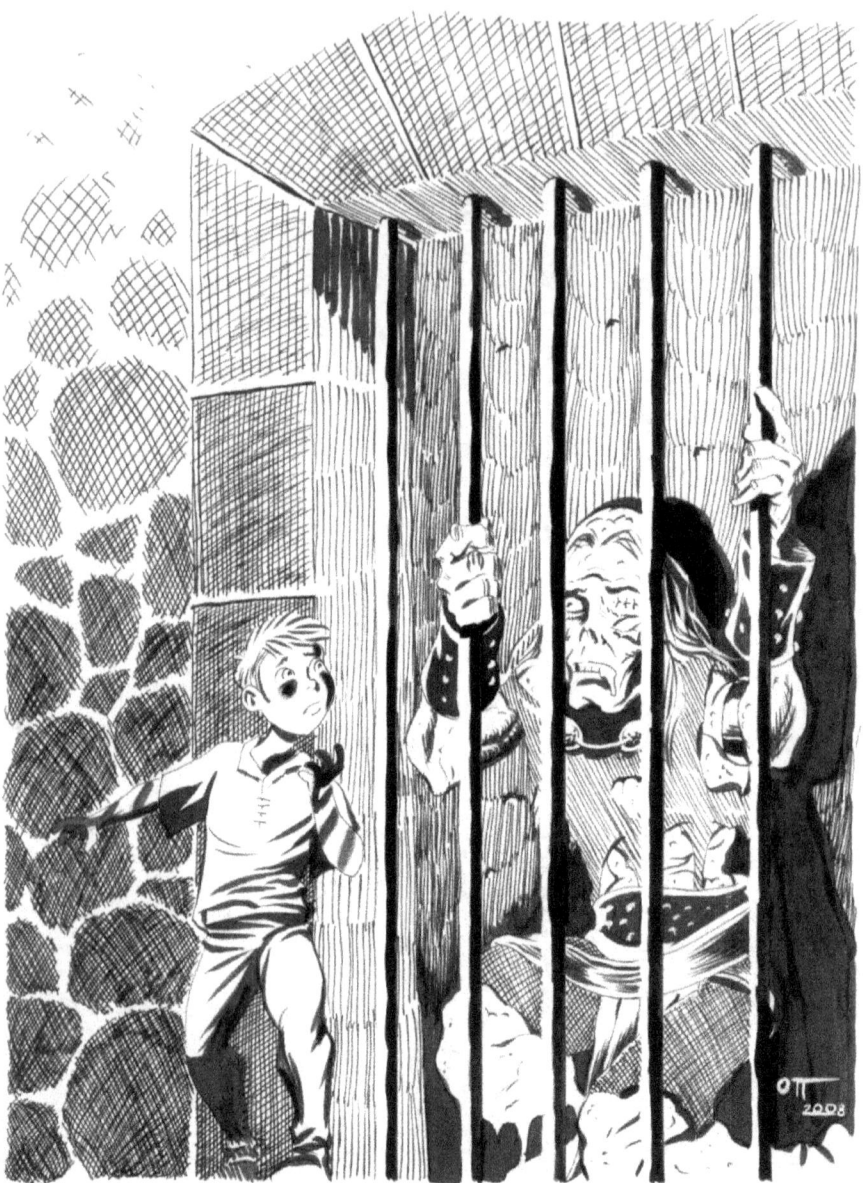

Bik and Korin

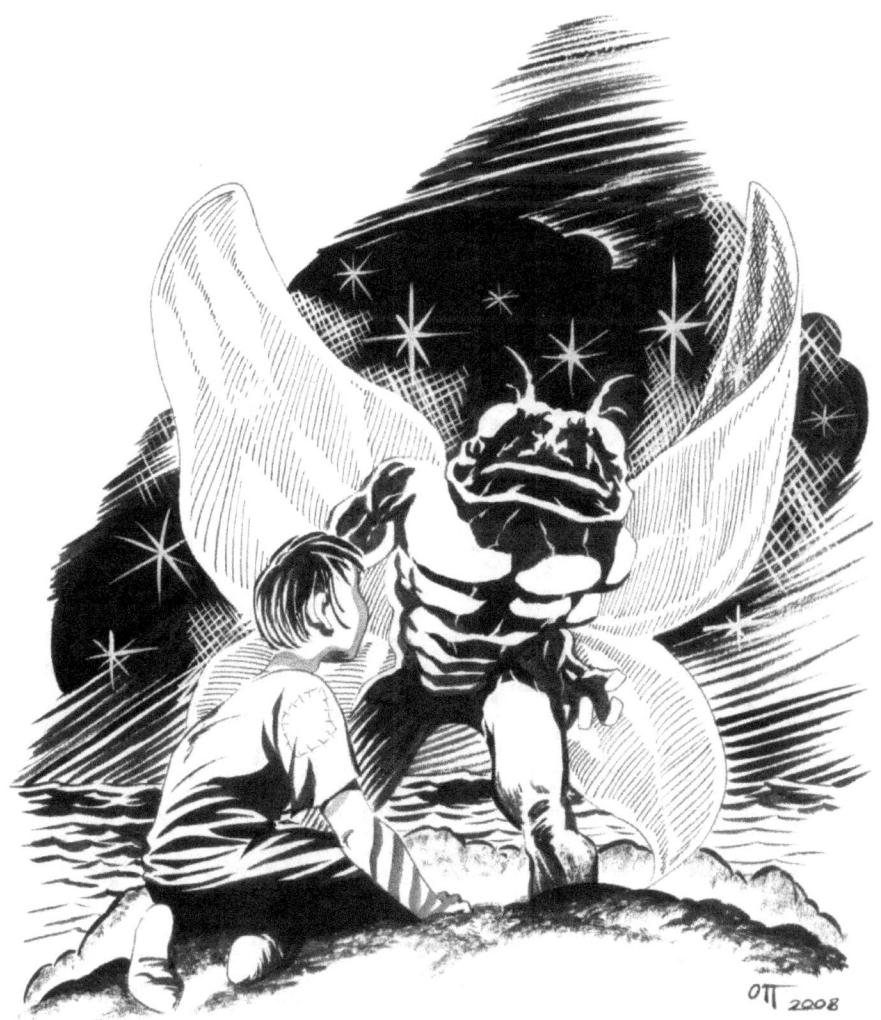

Bik meets an Altered Creature

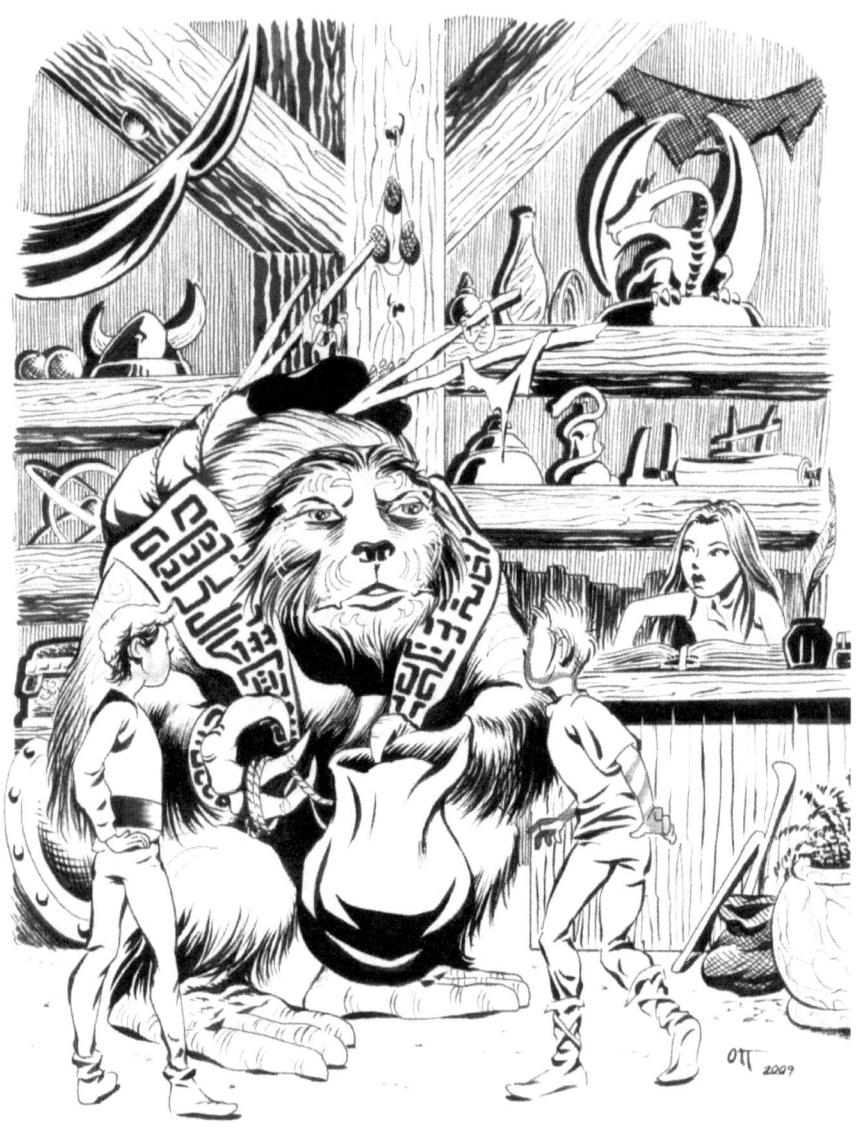

Pruva visits Gaz, Bik and Faun at the "Dare to Trade" shop

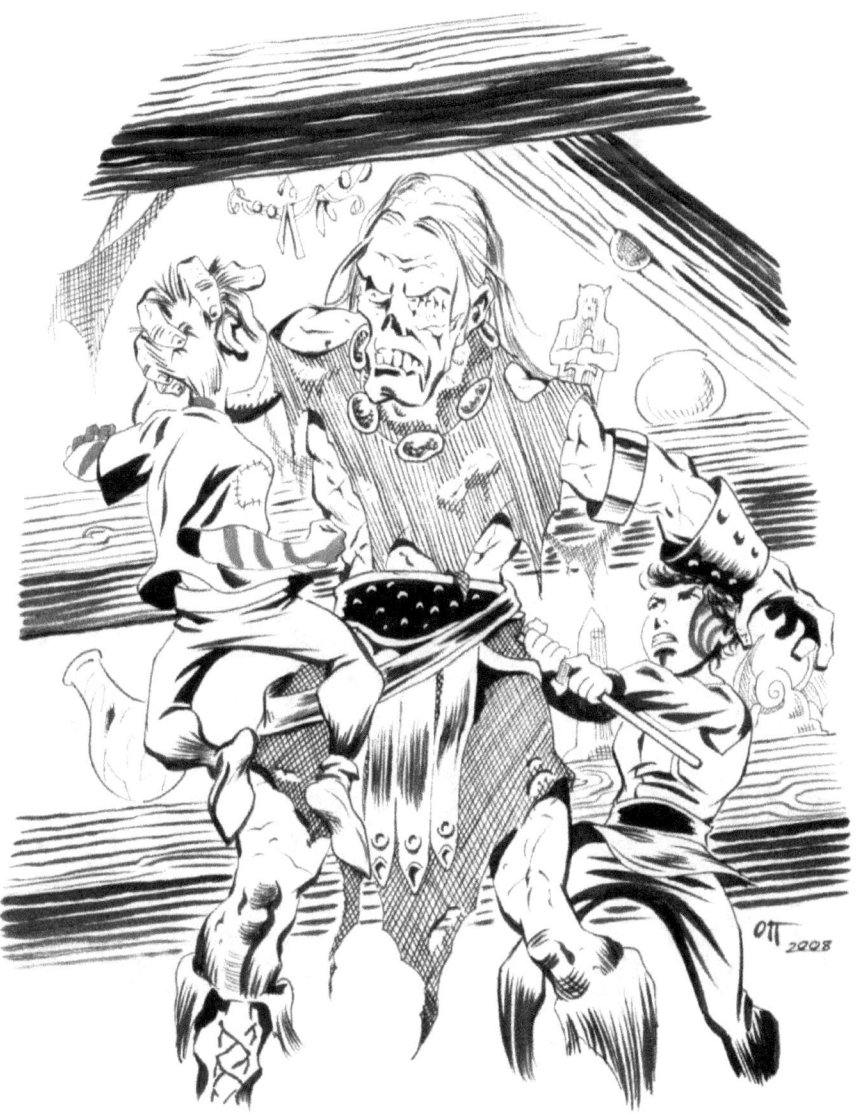

Korin searches for magic at the shop where Bik and Gaz work

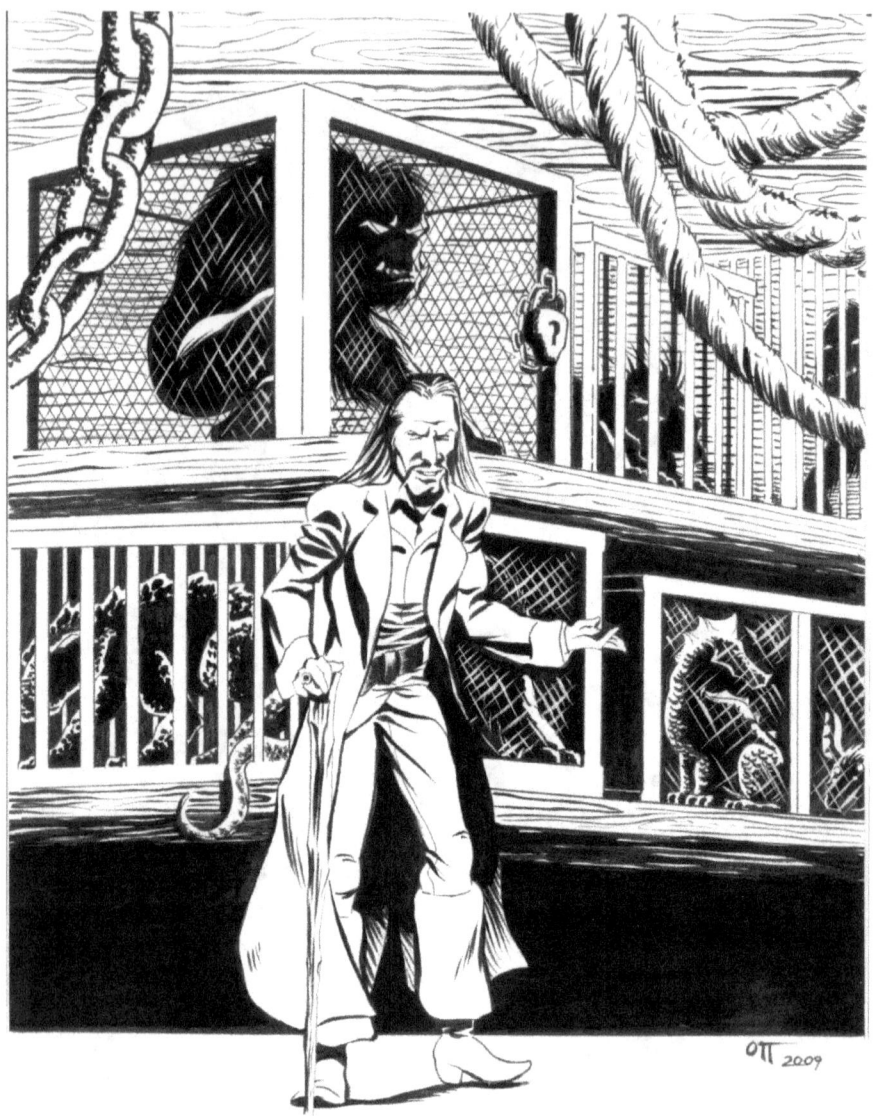

Malice Duprey and his caged creatures

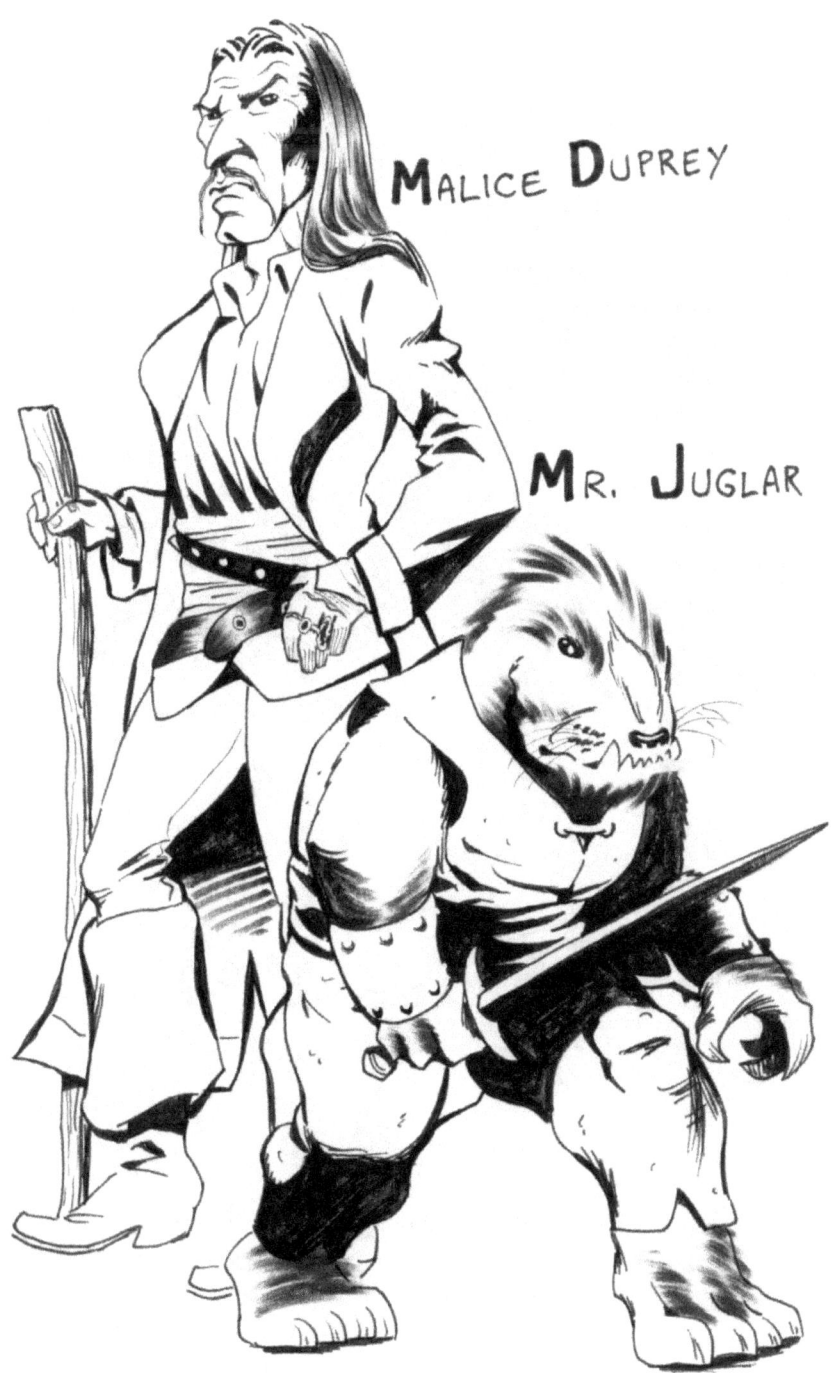

MALICE DUPREY

MR. JUGLAR

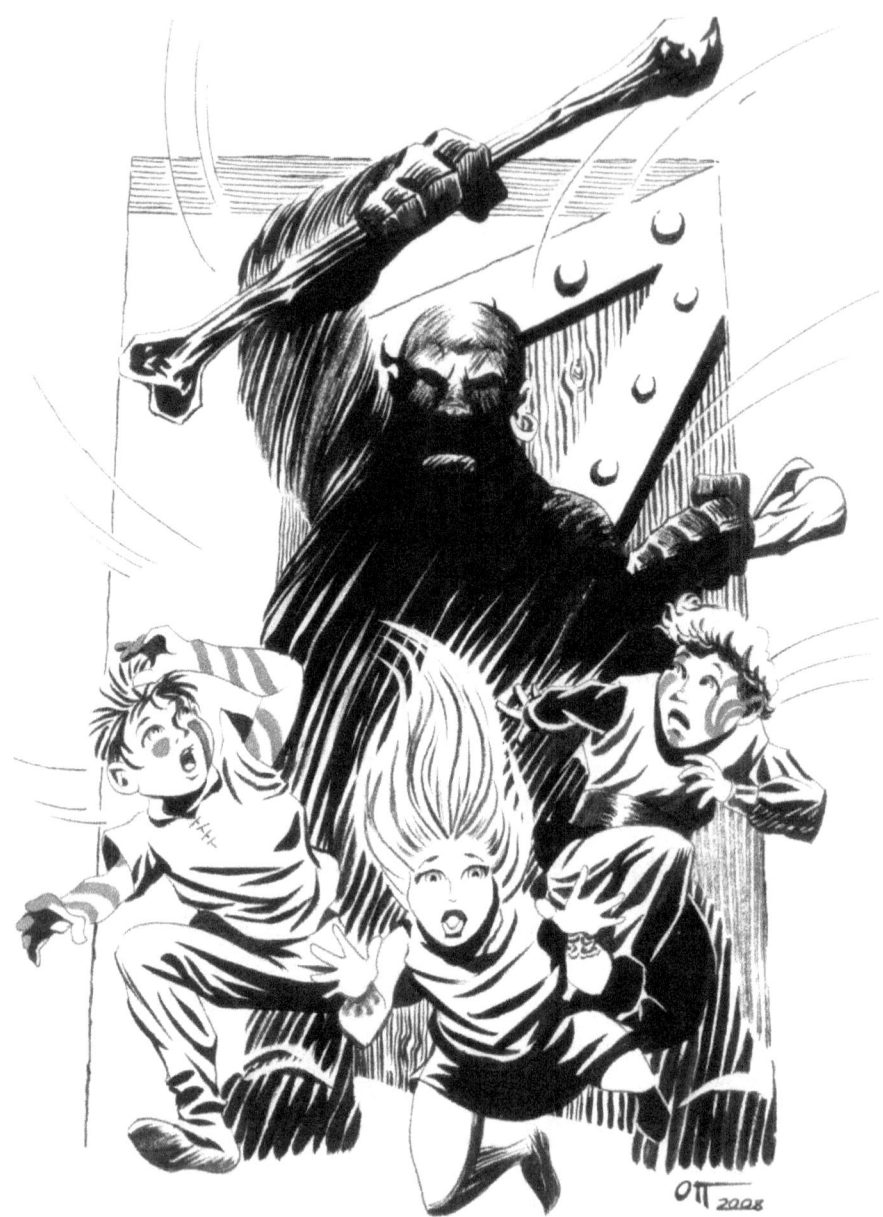

Bik, Faun, and Gaz
run for safety

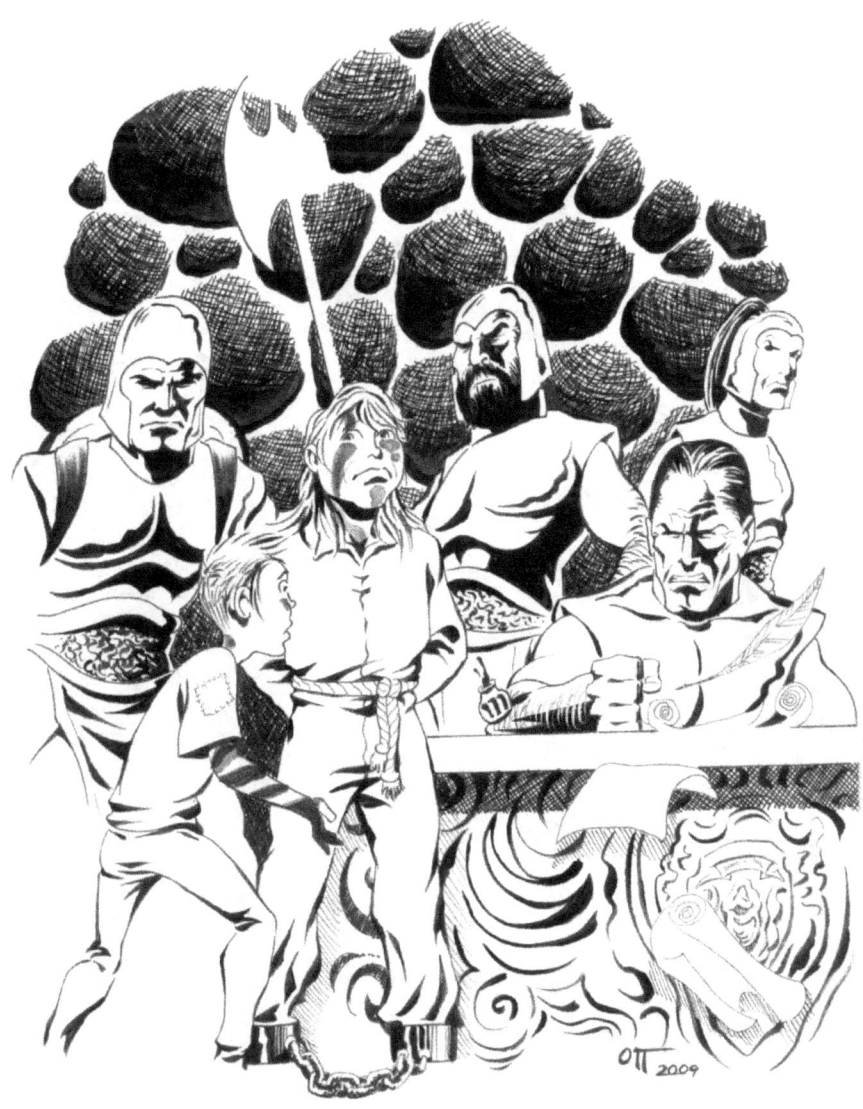

Bik tries to free his father

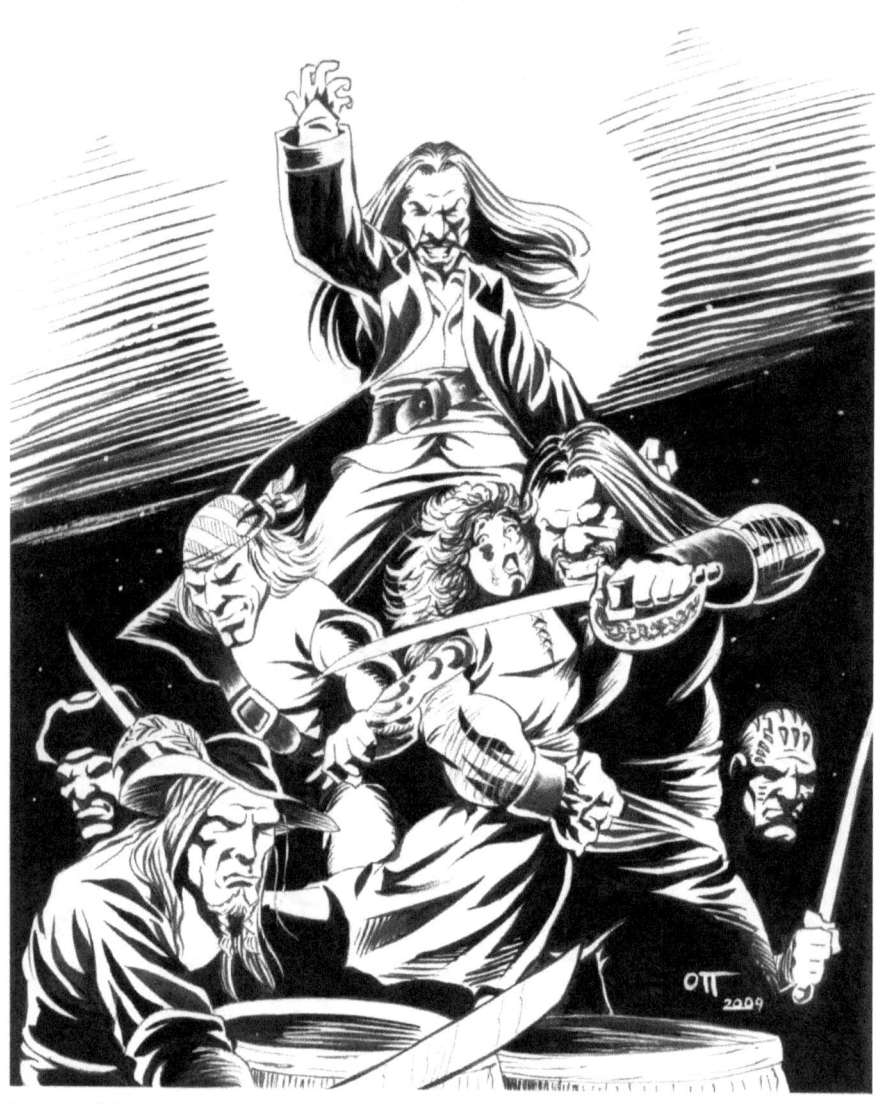

Malice Duprey and his Pirates

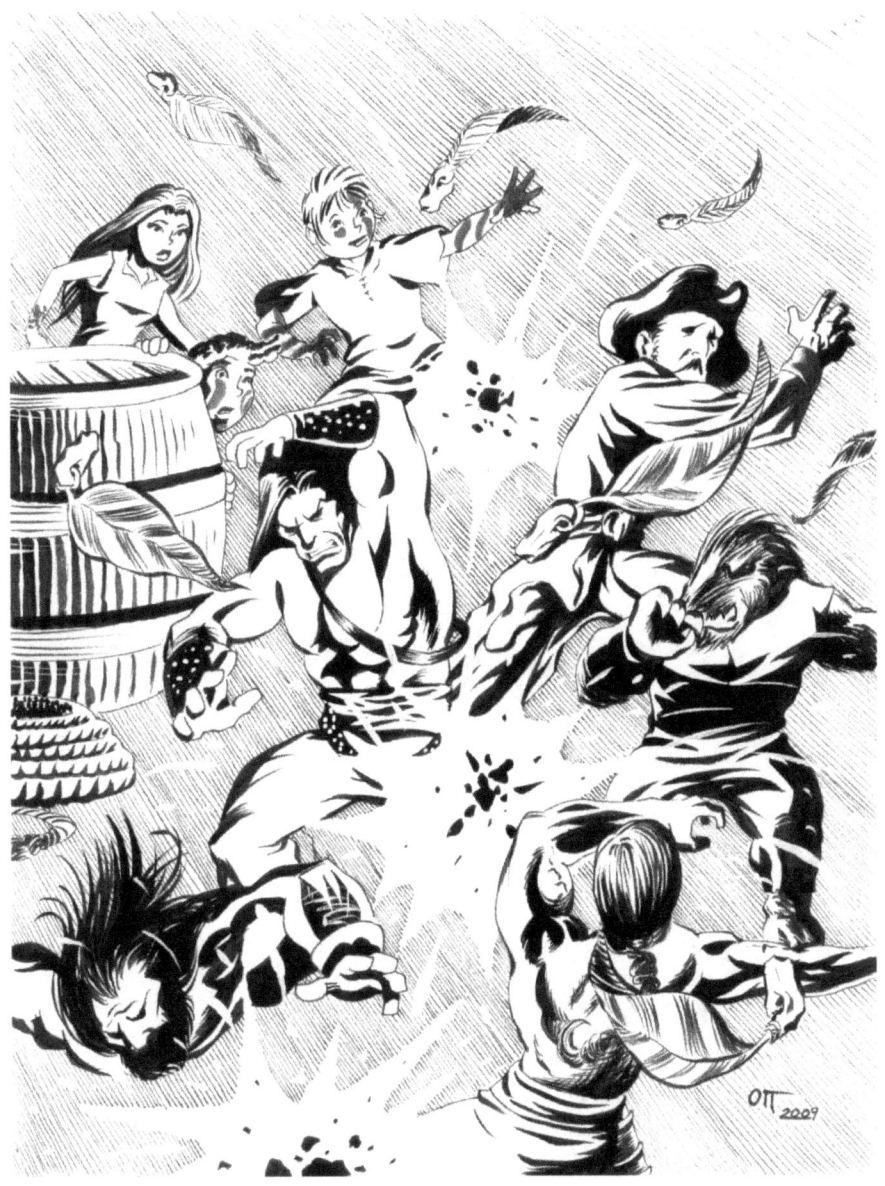

Bik and Faun use magic
to escape the Priates

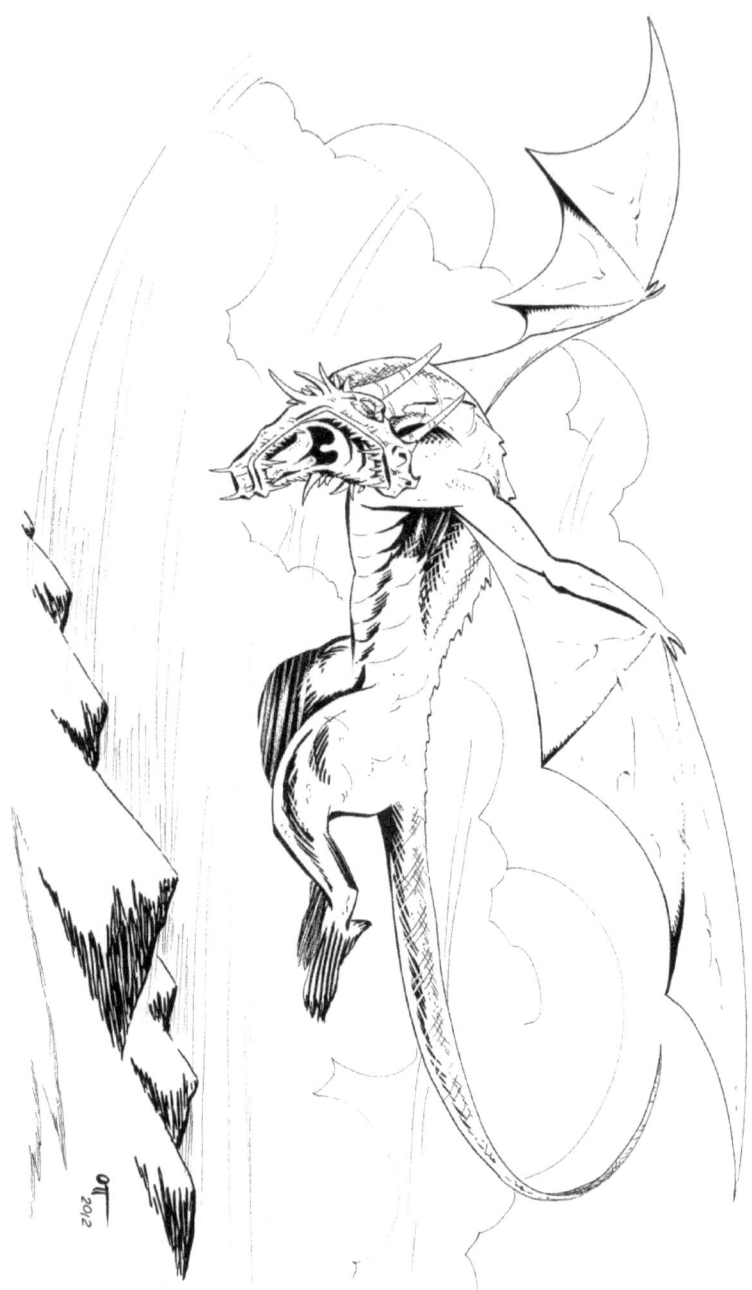

Draq flying high above

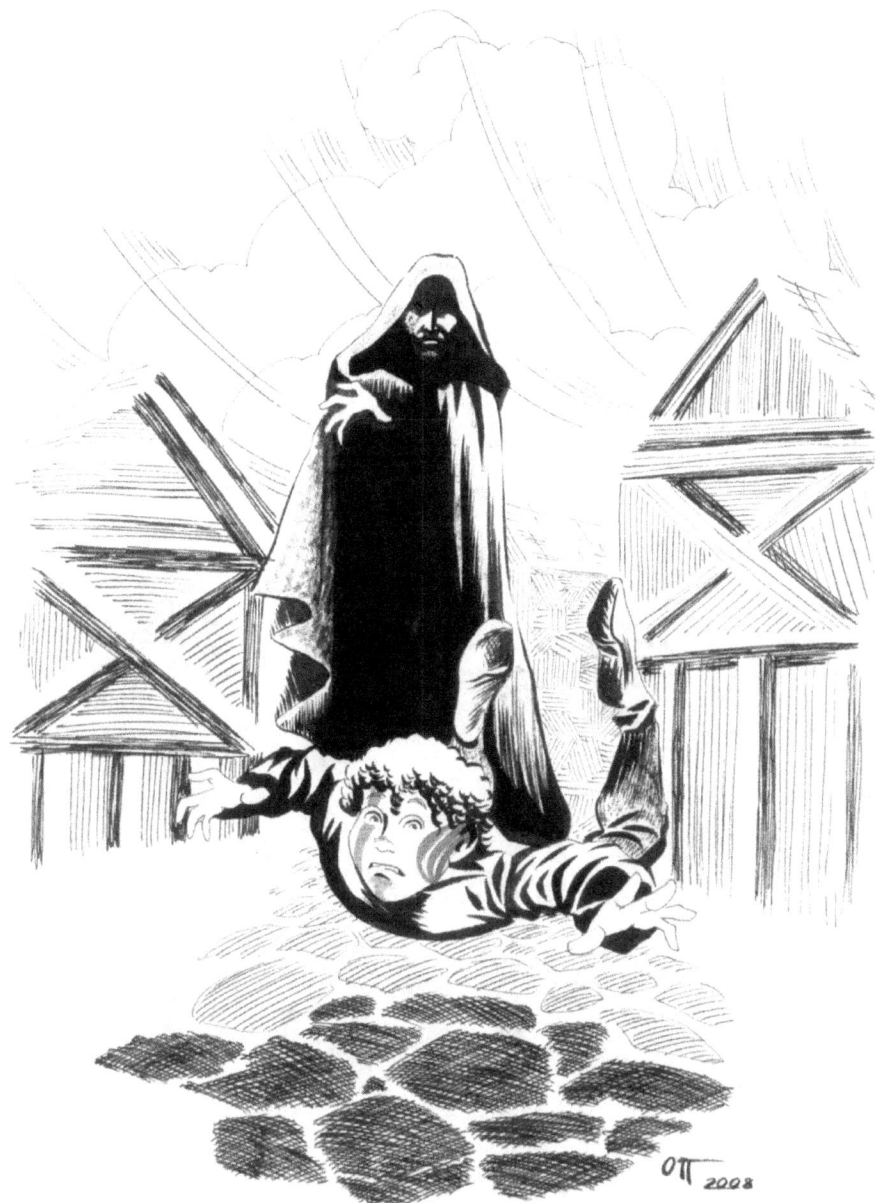

Ambrosius catches Gaz

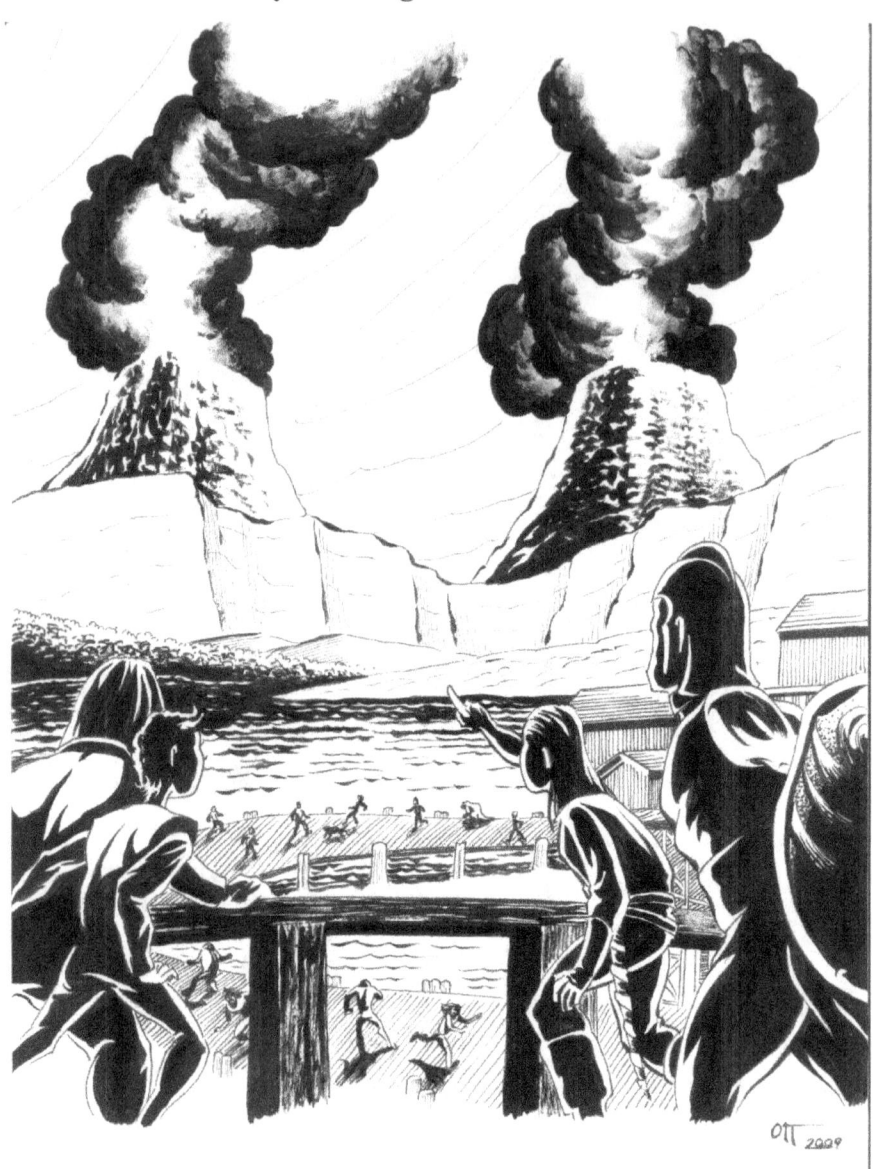

Valcanoes erupt near the city

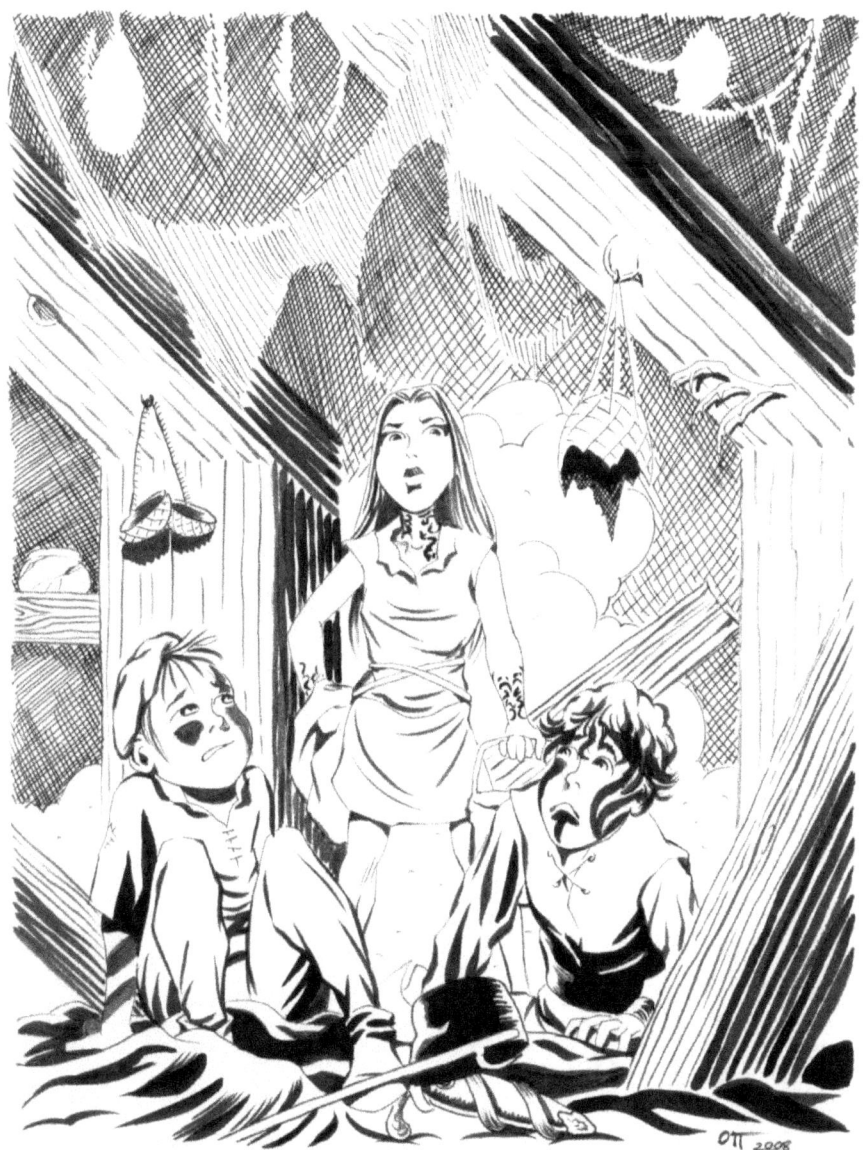

Bik, Faun, and Gaz win the day but mess up the shop

**Altered Creatures Epic Adventures
continues with the following books:**

**Thorik Dain Series
(Young Adult and Adult)**
Treasure of Sorat (short story prequel)
Fate of Thorik
Sacrifice of Ericc
Essence of Gluic
Rise of Rummon
Prey of Ambrosius
Plea of Avanda

**Nums of Shoreview Series
(Pre-teen, Ages 7 to 12)**
Stolen Orb
Unfair Trade
Slave Trade
Baka's Curse
Haunted Secrets
Rodent Buttes

Read free stories and further adventures at
www.AlteredCreatures.com

www.ingramcontent.com/pod-product-compliance
Lightning Source LLC
Chambersburg PA
CBHW071017180526
45168CB00003B/1451